CAMBRIDGE TEXTBOOKS IN LINGUISTICS

General Editors: B. COMRIE, C. J. FILLMORE, R. LASS, D. LIGHTFOOT,
J. LYONS, P. H. MATTHEWS, R. POSNER, S. ROMAINE, N. V. SMITH,
N. VINCENT

D0819420

THE PHYSICS OF SPEECH

THE PHYSICS OF SPEECH

D. B. FRY

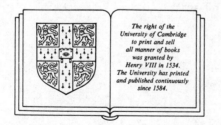

The right of the
University of Cambridge
to print and sell
all manner of books
was granted by
Henry VIII in 1534.
The University has printed
and published continuously
since 1584.

CAMBRIDGE UNIVERSITY PRESS

CAMBRIDGE

NEW YORK   PORT CHESTER

MELBOURNE   SYDNEY

Published by the Press Syndicate of the University of Cambridge
The Pitt Building, Trumpington Street, Cambridge CB2 1RP
40 West 20th Street, New York, NY 10011, USA
10 Stamford Road, Oakleigh, Melbourne 3166, Australia

© Cambridge University Press 1979

First published 1979
Reprinted 1980, 1982, 1984, 1985, 1987, 1989

Printed in Great Britain at the University Press, Cambridge

Library of Congress cataloguing in publication data
Fry, Dennis Butler.
The physics of speech.
(Cambridge textbooks in linguistics)
Includes index.
1. Speech. 2. Sound-waves. I. Title.
QP306.F8   1979   612'.78   78–56752

ISBN 0 521 22173 0 hard covers
ISBN 0 521 29379 0 paperback

CONTENTS

PHONETIC SYMBOLS

Vowels	Key-words	Consonants	Key-words
iː	heed	p	pie
i	hid	b	buy
e	head	t	tie
a	had	d	die
aː	hard	k	kite
o	hod	g	guy
oː	hoard	tʃ	chide
u	hood	dʒ	jive
uː	who	tr	try
ʌ	hub	dr	dry
əː	herb	f	fie
ə	abide	v	vie
ei	hay	θ	thigh
ou	hoe	ð	thy
ai	high	s	sigh
au	how	z	zoo
oi	boy	ʃ	shy
iə	hear	ʒ	measure
eə	hair	h	high
uə	tour	m	my
		n	nigh
		ŋ	king
		j	you
		w	why
		l	lie
		r	rye

I

The speech chain

When two people are talking to each other, a great deal of activity of many different kinds is going on in both of them. The most vital part of this is taking place in their brains because this is where they have stored away all the knowledge about the language they are using, which is indispensable for communication by speech. In the speech centres of the brain we carry information about the phonological system of the language, that is the significant differences in speech sounds, in intonation and in rhythmic pattern, about the grammatical and syntactic procedures which govern our speech and the very extensive vocabulary that we call on when we are taking in speech or sending it out. The whole time anyone is speaking, his brain is busy putting into language form whatever it is he wants to say, that is it is choosing words from the dictionary carried in the cortex, arranging the form of the remark and putting the words in the appropriate order, inserting the grammatical elements and form words, and stringing together the phonemes which make up the message. In addition to all this purely linguistic work, his brain is sending out a continuous flow of operating instructions which go to the many different muscles involved in making the skilled movements of speech. These instructions issue from the brain in the shape of nerve impulses which go to broadly three muscle systems: the breathing muscles in the chest and trunk, the muscles of the larynx, used in phonation, and the muscles of the head and neck which take part in the articulation of speech sounds. The resulting movements of the various parts of the speech mechanism generate the sound waves of speech which flow out in all directions from the speaker, some of the acoustic energy falling on the ears of the listener. Everything that is happening up to this point we can think of as the transmission phase of the speech communication, while all that happens subsequently is the reception phase.

During the transmission phase the message which the speaker intends to send out has appeared in four very different and well-defined forms: first as a string of language units, then as a chain of nerve impulses, next as a sequence of muscle movements and finally as a train of sound waves. The object of the reception phase is to reverse this process, to unwind as it were the series of changes the message has undergone in transmission. When the sound waves of speech impinge on the listener's ear they set up movements in the eardrum, the ossicles of the middle ear and the structures and fluids of the inner ear. These movements give rise to nerve impulses in the nerves which connect the ear with the speech centres of the brain. Here in the final stage of reception, the listener's brain reconstructs the sequence of language units originally formulated by the speaker's brain. The communication chain that is set up during speech is, then, neatly symmetrical since on the speaker's side it entails the conversion of language units into nerve impulses, of nerve impulses into movements and of movements into sound waves, while on the listener's side the sound waves are transformed into movements, the movements to nerve impulses and the nerve impulses to language units once more.

Speech generally appears to us to be some kind of unified activity but these successive transformations of a spoken message constitute the essential nature of speech; it is a series of changes. In spite of this we manage to talk to each other quite easily most of the time. This means that between all the different forms of a message, language units, nerve impulses, movements and sound waves, systematic correspondences or correlations are maintained so that the essential information does not disappear as it is conveyed from speaker to listener. The basis of this essential information is the language system which is known to both listener and speaker; this system dictates what sounds must be kept distinct from each other, what intonation and rhythmic patterns, and the articulatory mechanism is appropriately instructed so that differences appear in the resulting sound waves. These differences are perceived by the listening ear and provide the basis for decoding the message.

The study of speech involves before everything else the study of the correspondences that exist between the various forms of a spoken message and because the transformations take place from one medium to another, each level of speech activity calls for its own techniques of investigation. The linguistic side, with its dependence on memory stores and mental processing, is a psychological study; the action of nerves and muscles are a matter of physiology; the generation and transmission of sound waves fall within the realm of physics. The rest of this book will be concerned with this last aspect of the subject but it must be emphasized again that whatever we can learn about the physiology or the physics of speech is of real interest only to the extent that it can be related to the functioning of a language system. There are many facts to be learned about the physics of speech which have application to all language systems, particularly those which refer to the generation of sounds by the speech mechanism, but it is a matter of convenience to take a specific language as a framework for reference and for our purposes this will naturally be the English language system. The aim of the book, therefore, is to give an account of the physical properties of the speech mechanism and of its functioning as a sound generator, of the acoustic characteristics of speech sounds in general and of the principal correspondences between acoustic features and the elements of the English phonological system.

Sounds are physical events governed by very much the same laws as many other kinds of phenomenon to be found in the physical universe. They exemplify the effects of forces acting upon physical bodies to produce movements of various kinds. The criterion which separates sounds into a category of their own is not, however, a physical one since it is related to the human receiving apparatus: sounds are those physical events which give rise to the sensation of 'sound' in the human being, in other words the hearing mechanism is sensitive only to a certain restricted range of phenomena in the physical world. Sensations are themselves part of the psychological world so that the study of sounds inevitably links the areas of psychology and physics. It is true that the term *acoustic* is usually applied to the treatment of physical effects alone, but the word itself in its root meaning signifies relating to the sense of hearing. Speech sounds are a limited class of sounds and we have already seen that in studying the physical side of speech the principal objective is to establish the relations between the physical input to the ear, that is the stimulus, and not only the sensations to which it gives rise but also the further organization of those sensations in accordance with the language system.

In the world of sound, as elsewhere, some of the things that happen are relatively simple in character and others are extremely complex. We do not need any knowledge of mechanics to realize intuitively that to give an account of the working of a bicycle is a simpler task than to do the same for a motor-car with an eight-cylinder engine. The latter is more complex in the sense that more things are happening at the same time and that to specify the complete working of the mechanism would call for many different kinds of measurement and would involve measuring to much

3

finer limits. The sounds of speech are among the most complex sounds that exist in nature and to specify them is a correspondingly complicated business. The principles involved are relatively simple and can be grasped certainly without any previous knowledge of physics or mathematics, but in order to make these principles clear it is necessary to start from sounds which are very much simpler, physically or acoustically speaking, than the sounds which occur in speech; the majority of musical sounds, for example, are less complex than speech sounds.

In the following chapters, therefore, we shall begin with elementary acoustic principles, illustrated by the working of the simplest acoustic systems, and with the various ways in which sounds can be measured. We shall then go on to some of the more complex notions needed for understanding the working of the speech mechanism as a sound generator, the acoustic specification of speech sounds and the functioning of acoustic properties with respect to the language system.

2

The generation of sound

One of the facts of life which is rarely taught or even formulated is that it is not possible to get something for nothing out of nature. Whenever physical work has to be done, some supply of energy is required and the work actually consists in converting this energy from one form into another. The generating of sounds is physical work and it therefore depends on a suitable source of energy. Watching a large symphony orchestra at a moment when all the players are engaged is a good demonstration of the point; something over a hundred people are in movement at the same time, about three-quarters of them pushing their right arm back and forth, about one-fifth blowing and the remaining five per cent hitting things, using one or both arms. This constitutes the source of the energy which is being converted into the sound of the symphony orchestra playing *fortissimo*. If the sound is reduced until everyone is playing very quietly, it is obvious that much less energy is being expended, and if all the players rest, leaving the leader to play a solo passage on the violin, the amount is very much less still but energy must continue to be supplied by that one right arm.

The sound produced by the whole orchestra is very complex in the everyday sense since so many instruments are playing at once. It is not so easy to grasp that even the sound of the violin playing alone is a complex sound, in a technical sense which will be made clear a little later. In order to begin discussing sound generation we will take an example of the simplest kind of sound, physically speaking, that can be produced and that is the sound of a tuning fork. If you take hold of a tuning fork by the foot and simply hold it in your hand, it will of course not give out any sound, because the prongs of the fork are not moving, they are at rest. Energy must be supplied in order to produce sound and this can be done by striking the fork on your knee or on a table or, if the fork is large enough, with a small wooden mallet. Striking one prong of the fork just

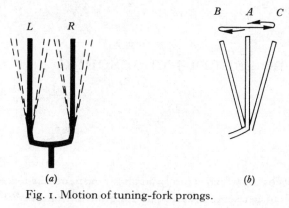

Fig. 1. Motion of tuning-fork prongs.

once will start up movement in the fork and set it into vibration in the way indicated, though very much magnified, in Fig. 1(*a*). The energy which you supplied by hitting the prong of the fork has been stored in the metal and is being expended in the to and fro movements of the left and right prongs. We can analyse what is happening more closely with the help of Fig. 1(*b*), where the right prong only of the fork is shown. Before it is struck this prong is at the position marked *A*, which is its position of rest; hitting it forces it from this position towards the left (in fact the two prongs move towards each other) as far as the position marked *B*. The distance from *A* to *B* will depend on how hard the fork is struck; the greater the force applied, the further the prong will move when it is first hit. The prong has been displaced from its position of rest and, in common with practically everything else in nature, it will immediately try to get back to this position so it begins to move back from *B* towards *A*. In the course of this movement it gathers considerable momentum and is unable to stop at *A*; it overshoots and moves out now in the direction of the point marked *C*. Here it is just as far from the resting position as ever, so it turns once more towards *A*, again overshooting and moving on in the direction of *B*, where it reverses direction in the attempt to reach position *A*, it overshoots, etc., etc. For our present purpose we can think of the distance from *A* to *C* as being equal to that from *A* to *B* (though it is not quite literally so) and so the prong of the fork repeatedly makes this journey from *A* to *B* to *C* to *A*. This movement is being mirrored by the left prong of the fork and it is these regular movements which constitute the vibrations of the fork and which give rise to sound. The motion of the prong from *A* to *B* to *A* to *C* to *A* makes one *cycle* of movement which is then repeated many times. The distance from *A* to *B* or from *A* to *C* is the *displacement* of the prong and though the distance will be very small, in suitable conditions it can be measured. If we were to stick a very small, light writing point (stylus) on the prong and to bring a sheet of paper up to touch this point when the fork was vibrating, it would draw a line (it would not be a straight line but a very shallow curve) which would give a measure of the distance from *B* to *C*.

We have said that these movements of the fork are regular, and this means that each cycle of movement takes exactly the same time as any other cycle. With the stylus attached to the prong we can check this quite readily. Imagine that we arrange for the paper to move along under the stylus at a uniform rate, the kind of arrangement used in a recording barometer. When the fork is at rest, the stylus will simply draw a continuous straight line along the paper, showing no movement to right or left. When the prong of the fork is vibrating, however, the stylus will trace the prong's motion from *A* to *B* to *C* and show how it progresses as time passes. The result will be a graph of the kind shown in Fig. 2.

The recording paper is moving away from right to left; the first thing recorded is the straight line which is drawn when the fork is at rest. Position *A* is shown in the graph by the dotted continuation of this line, so that at each moment when the curve meets this line, the prong of the fork was going through position *A*. When the fork begins to vibrate, the first move is towards the middle and a curve is traced from *A* towards position *B*; it then continues back to *A* and on to *C* and *A* repeatedly. One cycle of movement, you will remember, is the sequence *A–B–A–C–A*. The time scale is shown below the curve, with the instant at which vibration begins registered as time o. If you look at a tuning fork while it is vibrating, you will find it impossible to follow the movement cycle by cycle; one can only see a fuzziness in the outline, so it is obviously moving very fast. To make a time measurement we need a very small unit of time and that is why the scale shows the progress of time in milliseconds (thousandths of a second). One cycle is completed in 10 ms, half of this being taken up by the movement *A–B–A* and the other half by *A–C–A*. The movement *A–B* takes 2.5 ms and is one-quarter of the complete cycle. The whole cycle of movement is gone through many times (only the beginning of the vibrations is shown here) and each cycle takes exactly the same time, 10 ms. Because of the extreme regularity of the motion it is said to be *periodic* and 10 ms is in this case the *period* of the vibrations. This aspect of sound is more often expressed by calculating from the period how many cycles of movement are completed in one second. Since our tuning fork

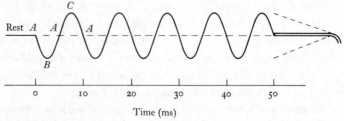

Time (ms)

Fig. 2. Curve tracing motion of tuning-fork prong.

takes 10 ms to perform one cycle, it will complete 100 cycles in one second and hence the *frequency* of the vibration is 100 cycles per second, abbreviated c.p.s. or Hz (after the German physicist, Heinrich Hertz). Frequency is the most important measurement that is applied to sound and it always means the number of complete cycles in one second. Tuning forks may have different frequencies of vibration and Fig. 3 shows two examples in addition to the time curve for our 100 cycle fork. The curves show the course of events after the vibrations have started and they begin, conventionally, with a deflection in the positive direction, that is towards *C*.

Time is again measured in milliseconds and the top curve is the one for the 100 c.p.s. fork in which each cycle of motion takes 10 ms. In the middle curve you will see that the fork has performed two complete cycles by the time the first fork has done one cycle, so the period is 5 ms and the frequency must be 200 c.p.s., twice that of the first fork. In the lowest curve the time relations are more complicated; at time 20 ms, this fork has completed three cycles while the 100 cycle fork has done two, so that its frequency must be 100 multiplied by $\frac{3}{2}$, that is 150 c.p.s. The period can be arrived at from the frequency by dividing one second (1000 ms) by 150 and this gives the value 6.7 ms (more exactly, $6\frac{2}{3}$ ms).

The first attribute of a sound that is measurable, therefore, is its frequency, but we must notice particularly that what is being measured is a property of the thing that is generating the sound. We are of course very much interested in the sensations that sound gives rise to, but it is essential to keep a distinction between the sound itself, that is the stimulus, and the sensation. If we listen in succession to the three tuning forks whose vibrations are represented in Fig. 3, we should certainly notice a difference in the sounds. The first would have the lowest pitch, the second the highest pitch and the third an intermediate pitch. The second would in fact sound exactly an octave higher than the first. We can

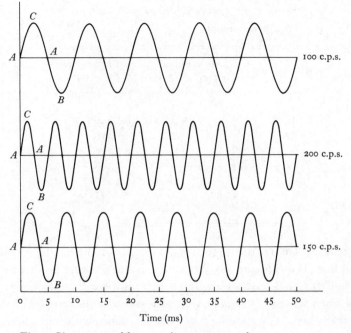

Fig. 3. Sine waves of frequencies 100, 200 and 150 c.p.s.

say in a very general way then that an increase in frequency of vibration leads to the sensation of a higher pitch. Increasing the frequency by 100 cycles produced an octave change in pitch, but if we now wanted to find a fork which sounded one octave higher than the 200 cycle fork, we should have to obtain one whose frequency was not 300 but 400 c.p.s., in other words we should have to double the frequency once more. This illustrates a general law which relates sensations with the stimuli which give rise to them: in order to add to the size of a sensation, it is necessary to multiply the magnitude of the stimulus. To add one octave in pitch, we have to multiply the frequency of vibration by two, and this is true whatever frequency we start with. What about the pitch of the third fork of 150 cycles? If we take the first sound, of the 100 cycle fork, to be the *do* of a musical scale, we should find that the 150 cycle fork sounded the *sol* above this *do*, an increase in pitch of a musical fifth. To effect this change in pitch, then, we have to multiply the frequency of the stimulus by $\frac{3}{2}$. Notice, by the way, that multiplying 150 c.p.s. by 2 will give 300 cycles as the octave above this note; this again is a fifth above 200 c.p.s. The musical diatonic scale is in fact a scale of pitch sensation in which the

TABLE I. *Frequency relations of the notes in the diatonic scale*

	Multiplying Factor	Note	Frequency (c.p.s.)
do	1	C	264
re	$\frac{9}{8}$	D	297
mi	$\frac{5}{4}$	E	330
fa	$\frac{4}{3}$	F	352
sol	$\frac{3}{2}$	G	396
la	$\frac{5}{3}$	A	440
si	$\frac{15}{8}$	B	495
do	2	C	528

notes are related to the frequency of vibration in the regular way shown in Table I. We can take any frequency as our starting point and call the resulting sound the *do* of the scale; by multiplying this frequency by the fractions shown in the table, we arrive at the frequencies for all the notes in the octave. They will be tuned in accordance with the *natural scale* or *just temperament*. Instruments such as the piano use a tuning which is an approximation to this, in which all the semitones are of equal size.

The example shown in the table provides two reference points which relate pitch to frequency: the frequency of 440 c.p.s. is that of the orchestral A which is sounded by the oboe when a full orchestra is tuning up; the middle C which corresponds has a frequency of 264 c.p.s. The radio time-signal is sent out on a frequency of 1000 c.p.s., a top C sung by a soprano has a frequency of 1056 c.p.s., the top note of a seven-octave piano is 3520 c.p.s. and its bottom note is 27.5 c.p.s.

Amplitude of vibration

With every cycle of movement the prong of the tuning fork is moving first to one side and then to the other of the position of rest. The distance it travels, as we have said, depends on how hard it is hit but is in any case relatively small. If we were to measure the displacement of the prong we should need to do so in something like tenths of a millimetre. The measure of the distance from position *A* to position *B*, or from *A* to *C* is referred to as the *amplitude* of the vibration; the amplitude of the tuning-fork vibration is indicated in Fig. 1 and shown more precisely in the graphs of Figs. 2 and 3, though we should need to add to these a vertical scale, for example in units of 0.1 mm, if we were recording actual measurements of displacement. It is clear, however, that in Fig. 3 the tuning forks are of three different frequencies but all have the same amplitude since the distance from *A* to *B* (or to *C*) is the same in each case.

Up to this point we have assumed that the distance from *A* to *B* was always equal to that from *A* to *C* and furthermore that it remained the same for cycle after cycle of the vibration. This is not the case physically and we can appreciate this very readily if we relate the amplitude of vibration with the sensation we get from the sound. If we hit the fork very hard we shall obviously hear a much louder sound than if we tap it gently, in other words the amplitude of the stimulus is linked with the sensation of *loudness*. It is equally obvious that after we have hit the fork, the sound will very gradually grow fainter and die away; the amplitude is decreasing until the prong of the fork eventually comes to rest and there is no displacement from position *A*. This must mean that the distances from *A* to *B* and from *A* to *C* are not exactly equal from cycle to cycle but the change takes place so slowly that, for the number of cycles shown in our graphs, the decrease in amplitude would not be measurable. A moderate blow will set a 200 cycle fork vibrating for perhaps two minutes before it comes to rest again and in this time it will have gone through 24 000 vibrations so the decrease in amplitude is clearly very gradual in that case.

Just as it is important to distinguish *frequency*, which is an attribute of the stimulus, from *pitch*, a property of the sensation, so it is essential not to confuse *amplitude* with *loudness*. We do not have a commonly used scale of loudness; we have only the very relative terms *forte* and *piano* and their derivatives. It is in fact a rather complex relationship that links amplitude with loudness, but we shall see later that it is basically a matter of multiplying amplitude to achieve equal additions of loudness.

Since amplitude refers to maximum displacement in a cycle of movement, its measure must be in terms of distance. Fig. 3 showed three vibrations of different frequency with the same amplitude. Fig. 4 shows the graph of vibrations having the same frequency but three different amplitudes.

Reading off the time scale, we see that in each case one vibration lasts 10 ms so the frequency is 100 c.p.s. The displacement is measured on the vertical scale in tenths of a millimetre. When we make this measurement we have to be careful to distinguish the direction of the movement away from the position of rest, so the upper half of each scale is given positive values and the lower half, negative values, the line marked 0 denoting the

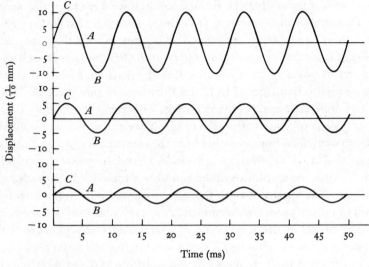

Fig. 4. Sine waves of different amplitudes.

position of rest, no displacement. In the top graph, the maximum displacement A to C is 10 tenths of a millimetre, that is 1.0 mm, shown in the positive direction, and is the same in the B direction, shown as -10. The amplitude in the middle graph is half of this, with C at 5 and B at -5, and in the lowest graph the amplitude is halved again, C at 2.5 and B at -2.5.

With regard to any vibratory movement, when we have determined its frequency and its amplitude we have gone a long way towards defining its physical attributes but we have been dealing only with the vibration of a tuning fork, which we said was the 'simplest' kind of sound, very far removed from the complexities of speech sounds. In order to be in a position to discuss more complex sounds, we shall need to consider a number of other factors which enter into vibratory motion.

Simple harmonic motion

Suppose that you hold a tuning fork by its stem with the prongs pointing to the ground and then strike one of the prongs. The fork will begin to vibrate and the motion of the prong, viewed in this way, will be seen to resemble that of a pendulum. The movement is many times faster than that of any pendulum we could set up with a weight and a piece of string but the movements are in other ways exactly comparable, as we

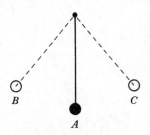

Fig. 5. Motion of a pendulum.

may see from Fig. 5. As in the case of the tuning fork, A marks the position of rest. In order to set the pendulum swinging we have to supply energy in some way but instead of striking the bob of the pendulum, we simply draw it aside from the rest position, let us say as far as position B. Gravity will now ensure that when we let go, the bob will at once begin to travel back towards position A. By the time it reaches A it will be moving so fast that it will overshoot and travel as far as position C; thereafter it will perform repeatedly the same cycle of motion as the prong of the tuning fork. The swinging or oscillation of the pendulum will be perfectly regular, that is to say each cycle of movement will take the same time and this will determine the frequency of the oscillations. This frequency will be much lower than that of any of the tuning forks we have considered; a pendulum set up with a small weight and a piece of string would not be likely to take much less than one second to perform one cycle of movement, that is the frequency of the oscillations would be 1 c.p.s., and the period might be much longer, depending on the length of the string used. We do not of course hear a sound when a pendulum is swinging because the frequency of vibration is well below the range needed to produce the sensation of sound in our ears.

The movement of a pendulum dies down comparatively rapidly; it might, for instance, complete 50 to 100 cycles of movement before coming to rest and we can readily see that the amplitude of the motion is diminishing, but notice that it is the displacement of the bob which alters and not the time taken for each cycle: this remains constant.

If we were to attach a light stylus to the bob of a pendulum, as we did to the prong of the tuning fork, and record its swings in the same way, we should obtain a similar graph, except that it would be spread out on a different time scale. Whereas one cycle of our first tuning fork took up 10 ms, one cycle of the pendulum movement might occupy a whole

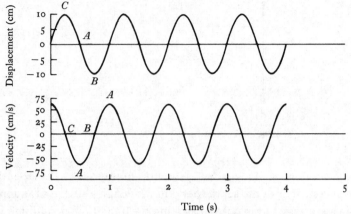

Fig. 6. Displacement and velocity curves of pendulum bob.

second, but if we make the adjustment to the time scale, then the curves will look the same, as we see from the graph of the pendulum shown in the upper curve of Fig. 6. Since the movement of the pendulum is easily visible to the eye, it obviously travels much further from *A* to *B* and *A* to *C*, as well as taking much longer over it than the tuning fork, so we need to change the displacement scale also and record distances in centimetres instead of tenths of a millimetre.

The technical name for the type of movement performed by both the prong of the tuning fork and the pendulum is *simple harmonic motion*. Whenever something carries out a cycle of movement in which displacement varies with the passage of time in exactly the way shown in all the curves we have so far looked at, it is an example of simple harmonic motion. The motion has a further property which we must now examine. Up to now we have talked only about the distance and the direction travelled by the bob of the pendulum or the prong of the fork at a given moment. Now we have to consider how fast the bob or the prong is travelling at a given moment. It is somewhat easier to see this in the case of the pendulum; the bob is swinging first to the left and then to the right so there are obviously two moments in each cycle when it reverses direction. At the very moment when it does this it must clearly be stationary, that is it has no speed at all. When it travels back towards *A* it gathers speed and is actually moving fastest when it passes through position *A*, and this is the reason for the overshoot. In talking of displacement we were careful to differentiate the two directions of movement, towards *B* or towards *C*, and it is essential to do the same with regard to speed, so we use the term *velocity* to denote speed in a given direction, again using the convention that velocity is negative when movement is towards *B* and positive when it is towards *C*. In the upper graph of Fig. 6 we have shown the bob of the pendulum as moving 10 cm from *A* to *B* and 10 cm from *A* to *C*. A cycle of movement therefore entails travelling a distance of 40 cm in 1 s, which means an average of 40 cm per second. But we know that at times the bob is going very slowly or is stationary and therefore it must reach a high velocity at other times to make up for this and in fact the maximum will be 63 cm/s. The lower curve in Fig. 6 is the graph showing the varying velocity of the bob of the pendulum and you will see that it is exactly the same shape as the graph of displacement but is shifted in time. When the displacement is maximum, that is when the bob is at *C* or *B*, the velocity is zero and when the displacement is zero, that is when the bob is going through position *A*, the velocity is at a maximum. In examples of simple harmonic motion, the displacement and velocity curves always have this form and there is always this same time relation between the two curves.

These relations between displacement, velocity and time hold good for motions of different frequency and amplitude. As the movement of the pendulum dies down, the amplitude decreases and therefore the distance travelled by the bob is less, but since it still takes exactly the same time to do one cycle, the range of velocity must also change and the shape of the curve is preserved. Thus, for pendulums oscillating with different amplitudes and periods (that is, frequencies), and also for tuning forks differing in frequency and amplitude, the basic shape of the graphs relating displacement and velocity to time remains the same; all are examples of simple harmonic motion. This particular shape of curve or *waveform* is called a *sine wave* and we will now look at the reasons for this.

Simple harmonic motion as circular motion

In discussing the action of both the tuning fork and the pendulum we have referred repeatedly to a cycle of movement which each performs. The word is appropriate not only because the prong of the fork makes the same movement many times, going round and round the cycle, but also because simple harmonic motion is equivalent to circular motion which is projected on a straight line. Fig. 7 shows a circle whose centre is the point *O* and whose radius is of length *r*. Imagine now that there is a point *P* which moves round the circumference of the circle at a perfectly

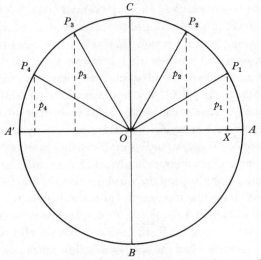

Fig. 7. Motion of a point on the circumference of a circle.

uniform rate in an anticlockwise direction. It goes round and round the circle and, because the speed is constant, the same time is required for every circle or cycle of movement. Let us look more closely at the progress of the motion as P performs one cycle. We will begin at the moment when P has just reached the position marked A on the horizontal axis. The point climbs up towards the position marked C and then moves down towards A', further down to B and then back to A once more. Since the movement is uniform, the same time is spent in travelling through each quarter of the circle and this will be one quarter of the period for one cycle. The distance that P has travelled at any given instant will depend on the angle which has been traversed; the full circle is 360° and each quarter, 90°, so when P reaches C the angle traversed is 90°, at A' it is 180°, at B it is 270°. A convenient way of expressing this angular motion is shown in the figure. Suppose that P has left A and has gone through an angle of 30° (P_1). From this position on the circumference we drop a perpendicular to the horizontal diameter of the circle and the length of this we will call p_1. The distance from P to the centre of the circle, O, is of course always equal to the radius r. The ratio p/r is the trigonometrical ratio called the *sine* of the angle at the centre of the circle, that is in this case 30°. We could take a ruler and measure the lengths of p_1 and r and work out the ratio but in fact the sines of angles are given in mathematical tables where we can simply read off the value of the sine of 30° which is 0.5. *P* moves on round the circle and at a later instant (P_2) it has gone through an angle of 60°; again we drop the perpendicular, p_2, which is naturally longer than before so that the sine of the angle has a larger value, 0.87. When *P* reaches position *C* it has traversed 90° and here the perpendicular coincides with the radius so the sine of 90° is 1.0. The sines of angles in the second quarter of the circle simply reproduce those for the first quarter; sin 120° = sin 60°, sin 150° = sin 30° and so on. At position *A'* the perpendicular disappears, that is it has the value zero and hence the sine is also equal to zero. For every angle traversed, therefore, the sine has some value between 0 and 1.0, growing in value from *A* to *C*, decreasing from *C* to *A'* and repeating this pattern in the lower half of the circle. For motion in the direction of *B* we again assign negative values.

We are now in a position to plot a graph showing the change in the sine of the angle traversed as time passes. To do this we have to decide on the period for one revolution and we also have to remember that equal angles are gone through in equal intervals of time. We will make the period the same as that of the first tuning fork that we considered, that is 10 ms (frequency, 100 c.p.s.). We will label the angle at any instant θ, and since we have only to look up the sines in a table we can assign to θ as many values as is convenient for plotting our graph, provided we keep to a constant increment in the angle. Table 2 gives sin θ for 10 steps from 0° to 90° and these will serve of course for all four quadrants of the circle. The horizontal scale is the time scale as before and the vertical scale has only to provide divisions for plotting values between 0 and 1.0 to, let us say, two places of decimals. The resulting graph is shown in Fig. 8.

By plotting the sines of angles from 0° to 360° we have arrived at the shape of the sine wave, which is also the waveform of the vibration of a tuning fork and the oscillation of a pendulum. To get another view of the relationship, try to visualize the movement of the foot of the perpendicular, *X*, continuously plotted as *P* moves round the circle. The movement of *X* will obviously be from right to left along the horizontal diameter and back again and thus will reproduce very closely the motion of the tuning fork and the pendulum.

The sines of angles are ratios and they do not therefore signify any measurement other than that of an angle; they do not tell us the values of times and distances. What then are the implications of differences in frequency and amplitude? The frequency of the vibration depends on the period of one cycle. We took as our example a frequency of 100 c.p.s. so

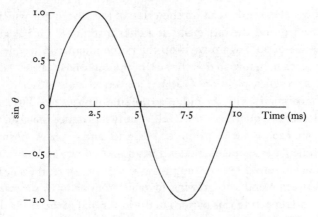

Fig. 8. Graph of the sines of angles from 0° to 360°.

TABLE 2. *Sines of angles from 0° to 90°*

θ (degrees)	sin θ
0	0
9	0.16
18	0.31
27	0.45
36	0.59
45	0.71
54	0.81
63	0.89
72	0.95
81	0.99
90	1.00

that P moved once round the circle in 10 ms. If the frequency were 200 c.p.s., as in our second tuning fork, then P would move round the circle once in half the time, 5 ms, and if we adopt the same time scale as in Fig. 8, we should need to plot all the sines from 0° to 360° in the space allowed for 5 ms; the wave would be exactly like the middle one in Fig. 3. Amplitude we know is a measure of distance travelled or displacement. The distance moved by X across the diameter of the circle is clearly equal to one radius to the left and one to the right of the centre; suppose now that the amplitude of this pendulum-like motion is decreased, then X is governed

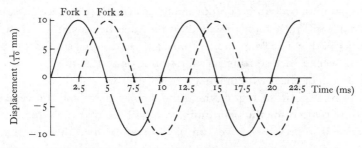

Fig. 9. Two sine waves with 90° difference of phase.

by a circle of smaller radius. If we imagine a smaller circle with centre O inscribed within the large circle we shall have a representation of a vibration with smaller amplitude. The distance travelled by X will be less, as we have seen, and also the distance travelled by P round the smaller circle will be much reduced since the circumference is proportional to the radius. Notice that the sines will remain unchanged since they are ratios; both radius and perpendicular in each case will be less than before. In order to record differences of amplitude in our graph of the sine wave, we should need to adjust the vertical scale; that is to say if the vertical scale in Fig. 8 were registering actual displacement and we had to plot a vibration with half the amplitude of the first, the point on the scale now marked 0.5 would represent a sine of 1.0 (i.e. 90°) in the waveform of the new vibration, and that marked −0.5 would represent a sine of −1 (270°).

There is one further aspect of the sine wave which can be best approached from the concept of simple harmonic motion as a projection of circular motion. Suppose that we have two tuning forks of the same frequency; we strike one and set it vibrating and then a split second later we start the other fork vibrating, so that the prong of the second fork moves away from position A just a few milliseconds after the first fork. We will assume that the amplitude of the second vibration is the same as the first so that this movement could be represented by the revolution of a second point P′ round the same circle. However, P′ is always just a little behind P. Let us suppose that the time difference is 2.5 ms; then P will have reached the position C on the vertical axis when P′ is at position A on the horizontal axis, a difference of just a quarter of the circle or 90°. Since the forks have the same frequency, that is the same period, this difference of 90° will be maintained throughout a single revolution and through all successive revolutions. Such a time difference measured in terms of the angle separating two vibratory movements is called a difference of *phase*. The graphs of Fig. 9 show the result of plotting the movement of these two forks, each with a frequency of 100 c.p.s., with equal amplitudes but with the second fork starting its vibration 2.5 ms after the first, that is being 90° out of phase with the first.

If you refer again to Fig. 6 where the displacement and the velocity curves are plotted for the pendulum, you will see that the same phase difference is represented; we can say therefore that there is a 90° difference of phase between the displacement and the velocity in this case because the velocity is zero when the displacement is a maximum and this relation is maintained throughout the vibrations.

Differences of phase may have any value between 0° and 360° and we shall return to this point in the next section but we might notice here the particular case in which one vibratory movement is going consistently in the opposite direction to another, that is to say the prong of one fork is moving from position *A* towards *C* at precisely the same time as the prong of the second fork is moving from *A* towards *B*. This is a difference in phase of 180° which is often expressed by saying that the motions are in opposite phase.

Addition of sine waves

So far we have dealt only with the simplest type of vibration or oscillation, simplest in the physical and mathematical sense because its *waveform* is a sine wave. Such vibrations may be referred to as being *sinusoidal* and the resulting sound is often called a *pure tone*. The sound of a tuning fork is one example of a pure tone; when people whistle they often produce pure tones, and a few musical sounds, for instance some low notes on the flute, provide further examples. It is very rarely in nature, however, that pure tones or sinusoidal sound vibrations are generated. Practically every sound we hear is not a pure tone but a *complex tone*; its waveform is not a sine wave but a *complex wave*. In a later chapter we shall look at the physical reasons for this but meanwhile we need to complete the discussion of waves and waveforms by discovering what property constitutes a complex wave.

The sine waves drawn in Fig. 9 represent the motions of two tuning forks, each of a frequency of 100 c.p.s., sounding together. It is true there is a phase difference but for many hundreds of cycles they will be producing sound at the same time and if we were listening to them we should certainly notice that the sound from two forks was louder than that

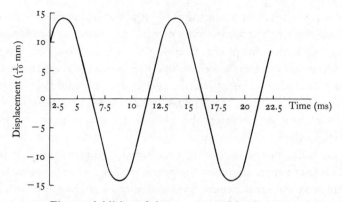

Fig. 10. Addition of sine waves resulting in a sine wave.

from one fork. This tells us that the combined sound must have greater amplitude, though we should not of course detect any change in pitch, that is to say the addition of the second fork would not affect the frequency of vibration. The increase in amplitude is due to the fact that sine waves can be added together. If we have the waves plotted on a graph of, say, displacement with time, we can literally add together the displacements for the two forks, provided we are careful to carry out algebraic addition, that is to say we must take note of the direction of the displacements and add them algebraically. The result of doing this with the sine waves of Fig. 9 is shown in Fig. 10.

One method of making the addition is simply to take a ruler and to measure the values of displacement for fork 1 and fork 2 and to add them together for as many values of time as we have the patience to fill in, but in order to illustrate the process we will take just a few of the salient points of the graphs. We begin the addition at the moment when fork 2 begins to sound, that is at time = 2.5 ms. At that instant the displacement for fork 1 (F_1) is 10 tenths of a millimetre and for fork 2 (F_2) is zero, so the sum is 10. Where the two curves cross at time 3.75 ms, F_1 is 7.1 and F_2 is also 7.1 so the total is 14.2, an amplitude appreciably greater than the maximum for either fork alone which is 10. After 5 ms, it is F_1 which has reached zero while F_2 is 10 and the combined amplitude is therefore 10 once more. There are points in time, one of them occurs at 6.25 ms, when F_1 is −7.1 and F_2 is 7.1, the algebraic sum is therefore zero and the combined wave passes through the horizontal axis. The sums of F_1 and F_2 form a pattern which is exactly repeated in the negative half of the cycle of the

21

combined wave; the result of adding these sine waves together therefore is a new sine wave of the same frequency but of greater amplitude and incidentally different in phase from either of the original waves. Whenever sine waves of *the same frequency* are added to each other, the result must be a sine wave of that same frequency, regardless of any differences in the amplitude or the phase of the original vibrations. There is one special case which might be considered an exception to this: imagine two sine waves of the same frequency with equal amplitudes but with a phase difference of 180°, that is they are in opposite phase. It will be clear that at any moment when the first wave has a positive value, the second will have an equal negative value and the algebraic sum will be zero. This will be true for every moment in the cycle, the two vibrations will cancel each other out and the result will be no sound. Such a situation would be difficult to achieve with tuning forks or with any other mechanical system but it can in fact be brought about electronically.

The principle of algebraic addition holds good whenever sine waves are added; the result is, however, very different when the vibrations are of different frequency. Let us suppose that two tuning forks, one of frequency 100 c.p.s. and the other of 200 c.p.s. are set vibrating at the same moment with the same amplitude of displacement. The two sine waves are plotted in the upper part of Fig. 11 on common scales. The second fork completes two cycles for every one of the first fork and the result of combining the two vibrations is represented in the lower graph.

The positive and negative values for the two forks add together to form some rather complicated variations in the sum of their movements and the result is certainly not a sine wave. A change of any kind in the relative amplitude of the vibrations or in their phase relations would alter the shape of the resulting curve but no arrangement of amplitudes or phase could produce a sine wave as the consequence of their combination. You will notice that the combined curve of Fig. 11 does show a repeating pattern since the waveform between time 0 ms and time 10 ms is repeated exactly between time 10 ms and 20 ms. The period of this repeated wave is that of the lower of the two frequencies in the mixture; we shall see that this is a point of some importance when we come later to discuss the ways in which sound waves are generated.

This example of the addition of sine waves is one of the simplest that we could have chosen: two frequencies, one double the other, with equal amplitudes and in the same phase. Most of the sounds we hear arise from much more complicated mixtures of frequencies. In Fig. 12 we see in the

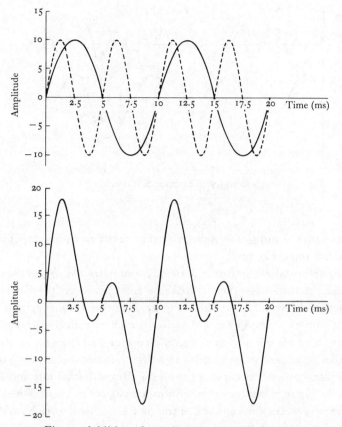

Fig. 11. Addition of two sine waves of different frequency.

upper curve the result of combining 5 different frequencies, 100, 200, 300, 400 and 600 c.p.s. to give a much more complicated waveform. The distinguishing feature of the sine wave is its perfectly symmetrical shape; the curve for the first quarter and the second quarter of the cycle is symmetrical and the negative half of the wave is the positive half exactly inverted. Any departure from this shape constitutes a *complex wave* and the sound with which it corresponds is a *complex tone*. It may not be immediately obvious that the lower curve in Fig. 12 is a complex wave but if you look carefully you will see that the rising curve in the first quarter of the cycle has a steeper slope than the falling curve in the second quarter; the negative half of the wave reverses this, having a more gradual slope in the third quarter and rising more steeply again in the fourth quarter. This graph was obtained by adding two sine waves of 100 and 200 c.p.s. in

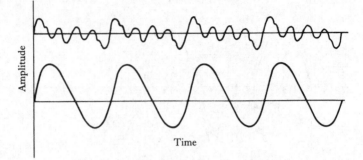

Fig. 12. Two examples of a complex wave.

phase but with the amplitude of the 200 cycle wave being only 20 per cent of that of the 100 cycle wave.

Any departure whatever from the strictly symmetrical shape of the sine wave means that the waveform is that of a complex wave, the vibratory movement is the result of motion at more than one frequency and the sound a complex tone. As we said earlier, practically all the sounds we hear in everday life fall into this class and certainly all speech sounds do so. In order to understand why this should be, we must look more closely at the physical properties common to all the things that vibrate and give out sound. There is obviously an enormous variety of them, when we think not only of the instruments of the orchestra, which are bowed or plucked, blown or struck, but also of the sources of the many noises which we would often rather be without. Because they differ so widely in character, they will be referred to as *vibrating systems*, a rather unwieldy term but one which serves as a convenient label, and as before we will begin with the simplest system, the tuning fork.

Physical properties of vibrating systems

When the prong of the tuning fork is struck, it is pushed out of its resting position, to which it tries immediately to return. The vibratory movement is the sequel to this need to restore itself to its former state, so this is clearly a property which is basic to vibration. The tendency to resist being pushed out of shape and to return as rapidly as possible to the resting position is the result of *elasticity*, a term used so nearly in its everyday sense as to be readily understandable in its physical applications. Materials and objects vary widely in their elasticity. When a tennis-ball is dropped onto a hard floor, it is momentarily pushed out of shape; the part of its surface making contact with the floor is flattened and the elasticity of the ball makes it resume its approximately spherical shape as soon as it can. The distortion of the material and the compression of the air inside provides it with a restoring force which makes the ball bounce. We might ordinarily think of a golf-ball as being less elastic than a tennis-ball, but a golf-ball when dropped will go back to its original shape even more rapidly than a tennis-ball, and a steel ball more quickly still; both of these therefore have greater elasticity than the tennis-ball. At the other end of the scale, a ball of putty when dropped will simply remain in its new shape, it is completely plastic (inelastic). The prongs of a tuning fork have a high degree of elasticity and when they are deformed by being struck, they tend to resume their original shape very rapidly.

Vibratory movement involves much more than simply a return to rest position, as we have seen; whatever is moving must overshoot this position in some considerable measure. It is the *mass* of the vibrating system which brings this about. We can think of the mass as being the amount of matter in a given object and also as the property which gives it *inertia*, that is to say which makes it tend to resist movement when it is still and to continue movement once it is in motion. Let us look again at the movement of the prong of the tuning fork, depicted in Fig. 1(*b*), in very slow motion. The right-hand prong is first of all stationary, kept in that state by the inertia owing to its mass. The blow which it is given applies a force great enough to overcome this inertia, to deform the metal fork and to set the prong moving. As it moves, elasticity provides a restoring force which increases with the distance from the resting position, *A*, until at position *B* it is great enough to counteract the momentum acquired from the blow and to bring the prong to a standstill. The restoring force due to elasticity sends the prong back towards *A* and inertia increases its momentum so that it overshoots position *A* and moves out towards *C*; once more elasticity supplies a restoring force and the sequence is repeated. Vibratory movement is therefore due to the interplay of elasticity and inertia, which are together responsible for the many repeated cycles of movement. At any instant the strength of the forces at work is determined by the distance from the rest position, that is by the displacement of the prong.

In an earlier section, when the notion of amplitude of vibration was introduced, we noted that vibratory movement cannot continue indefinitely and that the amplitude of displacement must decrease as time

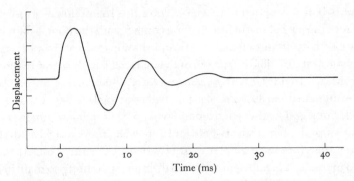

Fig. 13. Displacement curve of a highly damped system.

goes on. How long it takes for the vibrations to die down will obviously depend partly on the initial supply of energy; the blow which is struck, in the case of the tuning fork, governs the total amount of energy which can be used up in vibratory motion. Some of the energy is expended in overcoming physical forces which oppose the movement of the fork, in particular frictional forces within the metal itself and in the surrounding air. Vibrating systems vary a great deal in the degree to which they are subject to these frictional forces. If we hit a tuning fork a moderate blow with a small wooden mallet, the vibrations of the fork will continue for well over a minute, during which time the sound will be easily audible; if we give a blow of exactly the same force to a wooden table top, the sound, and that means the vibrations, will die down completely in less than a second. Both the tuning fork and the table top are displaced by the blow from the mallet and both are set into vibration. The difference between them is a difference in *damping*; the tuning fork has very little damping whereas the table top is highly damped. This technical term therefore means very much what one would expect it to mean: it refers to the property by virtue of which vibratory movement is rapidly damped down or reduced in amplitude. If we were to deal our standard blow with the mallet to a metal tray, we know that the sound would last considerably longer than that of the table top, but nowhere near as long as that of the fork. In other words, the damping of the metal tray is less than that of the table top but it is nonetheless fairly highly damped. The strings of a piano are set into vibration by the hammers; their motion has a considerable degree of damping and the sound dies away quite rapidly after the piano key has been struck. The piano includes, however, a mechanism for altering the damping of the system. Normally, 'dampers' made of felt lie in contact with the strings; the action of the 'loud' or 'sustaining' pedal lifts these dampers off the strings so that the vibrations continue much longer after the blow has been struck. The cymbals used in an orchestra are usually set in motion by clashing them together; although they are essentially metal plates, they are so designed as to have comparatively low damping and when the percussion player wants them to give out a short-lived sound, he applies artificial damping by bringing the edges into contact with his chest.

All the waveforms shown so far illustrate the motion of systems with very little damping, such as the tuning fork, and consequently no decrease of amplitude appears even after a number of cycles (see Fig. 3). If a force is applied to a highly damped system, the result is a waveform of the type shown in Fig. 13 in which the amplitude of the wave dies down very rapidly after the initial disturbance and the whole system returns to the rest position after a cycle or two of motion.

3

The propagation of sound waves

A tuning fork which is set into vibration gives out a sound which we hear if we are reasonably near to it, so it is clear that the effects of the movement of the prongs travel outwards from the fork in some way. In this chapter we shall look at the principles which govern the travelling of sound waves and at the various ways in which wave-motions may be propagated or transmitted.

The waves with which we are most familiar are those which can be seen on the surface of water. If a stone were dropped neatly into the middle of a perfectly still pond, we should see ripples begin to spread outwards in all directions towards the edge of the pond. Seen from above these ripples would appear as concentric circles. After some time the disturbance which took place in the middle of the pond would affect the surface of the water some distance away, in other words the wave-motion would have travelled from the middle towards the edge of the pond. Without thinking about the matter very closely, we may well be inclined to believe that this means that drops of water which started out in the middle of the pond have progressed towards the edge, but this is not of course the case. Suppose that something very light, such as a small cork, were floating on the water before the stone was dropped; when the ripples reached it, it would simply move rhythmically up and down as successive waves passed through the spot, without getting any nearer to the edge of the pond. The particles of water which form the surface of the pond are moving in exactly the same way as the cork, that is to say an individual particle of water is moving vertically up and down, as is shown in Fig. 14, in response to the disturbance caused by the progress of the waves.

Two questions at once suggest themselves: why should the water particle move up and down in this way and, if it does, how does this give rise to the apparent wave-motion across the surface of the pond? The first of these questions has been answered in the previous chapter, for we saw

Fig. 14. Representation of a water wave – transverse motion.

that the prong of the tuning fork, when displaced from its position of rest, tended to return to this position and this means that the particles of metal which make up the fork all have this tendency. The property is shared by every kind of particle we can think of, not only those which constitute solids but also those which form liquids and gases. The surface layer of the water is comprised of particles each of which, when displaced, tries to restore itself to the rest position. Like the particles of metal in the fork, they too have inertia which causes them to overshoot and to go too far in the reverse direction, thus setting up an oscillatory or vibratory movement analogous to that of the tuning fork. It is because air particles behave in much the same way that sound waves can be set up in the air.

In answering the question as to why the wave travels across the surface of the water, a second homely example may be helpful. If a length of fairly substantial rope is tied to a post at one end and the other end is held in the hand, a quick jerk of the hand upwards and downwards will produce a wave-motion in the rope which travels away towards the post. It is clear of course in this case that no particle of rope moves towards the post. Again the particles move only up and down but it is also easy to see that the travelling of the wave is due to the fact that all the particles are connected together; the particles actually in the hand are forced into motion directly, but those at successive points along the length of the rope are moved through their connection with adjacent particles and they do so with a time lag which increases as we get further from the hand. Notice that the up-and-down motion of each particle is due to the property already noted, the tendency to restore itself to the position of rest and the inertia which makes it overshoot, but the force which sets it in motion is applied to it by the movement of the particle next to it, on the side of the hand. The same principles are at work in the case of the water wave, although we now have a flat surface and hence an extra spatial dimension. From the point where the stone is dropped, thus producing motion of the particles at the centre of the pond's surface, force is transferred from particle to particle, causing vertical movement of the particles and an apparent wave-motion which travels horizontally in all directions. If we took an instantaneous photograph of the pond's surface in such a way as

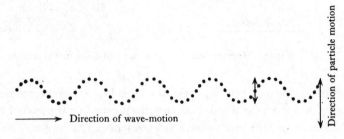

Fig. 15. Transverse wave.

to show the relative positions of successive particles over some small stretch of the surface, we should find them disposed in the way shown in Fig. 15.

The wave-motion progresses from left to right horizontally while each particle moves vertically up and down, the maximum extent of this movement, that is its amplitude, being indicated by the smaller vertical arrow. Because the particle movement is in a direction at right angles to the direction in which the wave is travelling, such a vibratory motion is called a *transverse* wave. It is clear from Fig. 15 that the water wave closely resembles the form of the sine wave and therefore the motion of the particles is following the same laws as those in our earlier examples of pure tones, though the frequency is not in the audible range. Transverse waves may be set up on the surface of a liquid or in some solids, as we saw in the case of the stretched rope, but in general they represent the more exceptional type of wave-motion. They cannot be set up, for example, in a gas and thus sound waves in air, which will be our major concern, must be wave-motions of another type.

An alternative to the transverse wave, in which particle movement is at right angles to the direction in which the wave travels, is a wave in which particles oscillate back and forth along the line of the travelling wave, a state of affairs which is at first rather hard to visualize. Imagine first of all that row *A* in Fig. 16 represents adjacent air particles lying at rest and in line with each other. Particle number 1 happens to be next to the prong of a tuning fork which is set vibrating, with the result that particle 1 is alternately displaced to the right and to the left of its resting position, in the way shown in row *B*. Air particles affect each other when they move, just as the particles of the water and the rope did, but they do so in a rather special way. When particle 1 moves to the right, it comes close to number

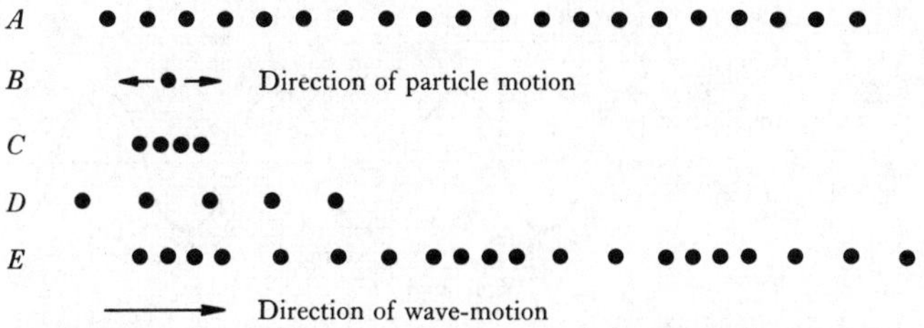

Fig. 16. Particle motion in the path of a longitudinal wave.

2 which is forced to move up on number 3, which moves up on 4 and so on, in the way indicated in row *C*. This crowding together of the particles is a state of compression, there is a minute rise in air pressure, and with the passage of time a wave of compression travels to the right through successive particles. Meanwhile the prong of the fork has moved to the left, thus making more room to the right and creating a minute drop in air pressure so that particle number 1 moves to the left. The particles near the prong are now spaced more widely than in the rest position and the wave of compression is succeeded by a wave of rarefaction, the condition shown in row *D*, which in turn travels to the right. Notice that the waves of compression and rarefaction are timed by the movement of the prong of the fork and therefore the frequency of the wave-motion in the air is the same as that of the fork. One move to the right and one to the left constitute a cycle of tuning-fork motion; one compression followed by one rarefaction will make up one cycle of the sound wave in air, and if the fork has a frequency of 100 cycles, it will take 1/100 s for the compression and rarefaction to pass through a given point in the air.

An instantaneous picture of the disposition of the air particles in the path of the wave would show a situation something like that illustrated in row *E* of Fig. 16. A moving film of particle movement would make it clear that each particle moves only to right and left and that the wave-motion itself travels from left to right. For this reason such waves are called *longitudinal* waves. All sound waves which reach our ears arrive in the form of longitudinal waves. For the sake of simplicity, this type of wave-motion has been illustrated with particles which lie on a single line. When a sound is generated, the sound waves travel outwards from the source in all directions. Just as the stone dropped in the pond started up concentric circles of wave movement on the surface of the water, so the tuning fork or any other sound source radiates sound waves in an expanding sphere, since atmospheric space is three dimensional. The sound waves travel

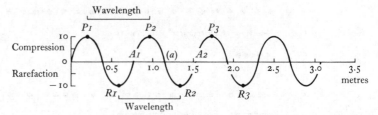

Fig. 17. Wave of compression and rarefaction, showing wavelength.

along every possible radius of this sphere and in every case the particle motion is parallel to the direction of propagation of the wave, that is they are longitudinal waves.

From the instantaneous picture of the water particles shown in Fig. 15 it is easy to see that transverse wave-motion may be a sine wave. It is less easy to grasp that the same may be true of a longitudinal wave. We could indeed draw a graph of the displacement of a single particle with time and if the motion were sinusoidal the result would be a sine wave. But here we have the added complication that we are dealing with wave-motion which is travelling and it is more in keeping with the real state of affairs to view this in terms of compression and rarefaction of the air particles at any point in space and at any particular time. At a given point there will be a maximum of compression at a certain moment and this corresponds to the peak or crest of the sine wave. Some milliseconds later pressure at this point will have fallen to normal atmospheric pressure and will decrease still further until a maximum of rarefaction is reached, corresponding to the trough or maximum negative value of the sine wave. Thus a graph of the rise and fall of air pressure at a single point in space will again yield a sine wave. Fig. 16 *E* shows, however, that variations in pressure are laid out in space at a given instant and we can therefore plot a graph indicating the variation in air pressure with distance from the sound source. If the source were a tuning fork, this curve too would be a sine wave and this is illustrated in Fig. 17. Air pressure is measured on the vertical scale in arbitrary units, positive values indicating compression and negative values, rarefaction. The horizontal scale gives distance from the tuning fork in metres; it extends over just a few metres close to the fork and we have to remember that the curve refers only to a very short time, since the wave is travelling from left to right. At this instant certain points in space are at the same pressure: for example, P_1, P_2 and P_3 are all at maximum compression and R_1, R_2 and R_3 are at maximum rarefaction. The distance between successive points of this kind is the *wavelength* of the sound; it can be measured at any point on the curve so long as we are careful to take corresponding points. Thus the distance from P_1 to P_2 or from R_2 to R_3 gives the wavelength, as does also the distance from A_1 to A_2. In the last case there is an intermediate point where pressure is at the normal atmospheric level (a) but is about to fall instead of rising; the distance from A_1 to (a) is the half-wavelength.

Before developing this subject any further it will be well to review briefly the kind of phenomena we are discussing. If you are in a room where someone sets a tuning fork vibrating, you hear the sound of the fork because the movement of the prongs displaces the air particles close to the fork and the effects of this displacement are transmitted through the intervening air particles to those next to your eardrum, which in turn is moved by the sound wave. It takes time for the wave to travel; there is a time interval between the moment when the prong first moves to the right, say, and the moment when you first hear the sound. In a room this interval is very short, but there are a number of familiar examples which bring home to us that sound does take time to travel and particularly that it travels much more slowly than light. If we see a race started by a pistol shot some hundreds of metres away, we see the smoke of the shot and then, after an appreciable lag, we hear the sound of the shot; if we are watching cricket played at a distance, we may see the ball hit and after a fraction of a second hear the sound of the impact of bat on ball; during a thunderstorm we often see a lightning flash and can judge by the interval before we hear the clap of thunder whether the storm is far off or quite near. In all such cases we are aware that sound takes time to travel, in other words that sound waves have a certain *velocity*. Sound waves in the air travel at a velocity of 340 m/s or 1240 km/h (aircraft travelling at speeds above this are moving at supersonic speeds). Thus the sound of a pistol fired a hundred metres away would reach your ear in just under one-third of a second; a count of 3 seconds between a lightning flash and a clap of thunder would mean that the discharge took place just about one kilometre away.

Let us now return to the question of the wavelength of sound waves and see how it is related both to the frequency of the sound source and to the velocity of sound. We have seen that the waves of compression and rarefaction resulting from the tuning-fork movement are governed by the frequency of the fork; if this frequency is 100 c.p.s., the compression caused by the first swing of the prong to the right will be followed $1/100$ s later by a second compression wave which is due to the second swing to the right. Since the velocity of sound is 340 m/s, in 1/100 s the first compression will have travelled 3.4 m, that is to say the air particles 3.4 m from the tuning fork will be affected by the first compression just at the moment when the second is imposed on the air particles nearest the prong. Hence a distance of 3.4 m separates successive peaks of compression. The fork vibrates continuously, sending out waves of compression and of rarefaction at intervals of 1/100 s. Consequently in the air around the fork there will at any instant be a peak of compression every 3.4 m and similarly a maximum of rarefaction every 3.4 m. We have already defined the distance between such peaks or troughs as the wavelength of the sound, so the wavelength of a sound with a frequency of 100 c.p.s. is 3.4 m in air.

Suppose now that we replace the 100 cycle fork by one with a frequency of 200 cycles. The interval between successive compression waves will now be only 1/200 s. In this time the wave will have travelled 340/200 m, that is 1.7 m, so that peaks or troughs will be separated by this distance and the wavelength of the sound will be 1.7 m. To find the wavelength of any sound in air, therefore, we have only to divide 340 m by the frequency; thus the wavelength of a sound of 500 c.p.s. will be 0.68 m and of 1000 c.p.s., 0.34 m. The sound represented in Fig. 17 has a wavelength of just over 0.75 m (between 0.77 and 0.78). By dividing 340 m by this distance we obtain the frequency of the sound, which is 440 c.p.s., the orchestral A.

In all the instances of wavelength given so far we have added the qualification 'in air' and the values have been calculated on the basis of the velocity of sound in air. Sounds can be transmitted through other media, through solids, through liquids and also through gases other than air. The velocity of sound varies with the medium and hence the wavelength of a given sound depends upon this medium. In order to understand why this should be so, we need to modify the extremely simplified view we have so far taken of the structure of matter, whether solid, liquid or gas. The 'particles' of metal, of water or of air referred to above have been seen as minute quantities of matter linked together in some way which permits the transfer of an effect from one point to another. The usefulness of this idea can be increased by the addition which is illustrated diagrammatically in Fig. 18.

We can think of the matter we are concerned with, of whatever kind, as consisting of a series of masses, numbered 1–7 in the figure, each linked to

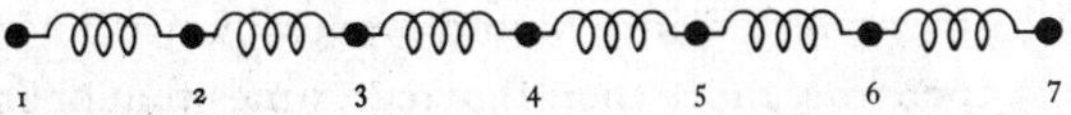

Fig. 18. Representation of coupled spring and mass elements.

the next by a coil spring. Any force along the line of springs applied to mass number 1 will cause it to move to the right and compress the spring joining it to number 2 and, if the force is sufficient, move mass 2 to the right. The first effect of the applied force may therefore be a wave of compression of the springs travelling to the right. But any spring which is compressed now has a restoring force which will move the mass back again to the left and each mass will provide inertia which will cause it to overshoot its resting position and so the springs will in turn be extended beyond their normal state, in other words there will be a wave of 'rarefaction'. Anything which can be set vibrating and any medium in which wave-motions can be set up has these properties, which also account for differences in the behaviour of different systems. If the masses are relatively great, the material will be heavy and also the momentum developed in vibratory movement will be large and the overshoot for a given force applied will be great, giving high amplitude of vibration. If the springs are stiff, then the movement of the masses will be rapid, elasticity will be great and the frequency of vibration will tend to be high, if the system is acting as a sound source. On the other hand, if the springs are slack, there will be little elasticity, a good deal of internal friction and hence a high degree of damping.

The velocity with which sound is propagated through a medium depends on the two properties represented by the mass and the spring. If the springs are very stiff, the velocity will be high and if the density is great, the velocity will be low. In the case of air, although the masses are very small, the springs are very slack so that waves travel slowly. On the other hand, in a steel bar, although the masses are much greater (that is the material is more dense), the springs are very much stiffer, so that sound will travel a great deal faster in steel than in air. This is demonstrated again by familiar examples: if one is standing on a railway platform, one may notice that the sound of an approaching train arrives earlier via the metal rails than it does through the air. The popular explanation of the expression hearing something 'on the grapevine' is that inmates of prisons pass information to each other by tapping on the water pipes and in this way messages cover a great distance much more rapidly than they would if converted into sound waves in air. The velocity of sound in steel is 5000 m/s, more than fourteen times that of sound in air. In a very dense metal such as lead, the masses are obviously great but there is very little elasticity and sound waves travel comparatively slowly, at about 1220 m/s. Sound velocities in liquids come in general, between those in gases and solids (the velocity of sound in water, for example, is 1520 m/s).

We saw earlier that the wavelength of a sound is dependent on the velocity of sound in the medium through which it is travelling. The time interval between successive waves is determined by the frequency of the vibration; from the velocity of sound we can calculate what distance will be covered in this time, that is the wavelength. The greater the velocity, the longer the wavelength for a given frequency; thus a tone of 100 c.p.s. which has a wavelength of 3.4 m in air would have a wavelength of 15.2 m in water and of 50 m in steel; the orchestral A, with a wavelength of 0.77 m in air, will have a wavelength of 3.45 m in water and of 11.36 m in steel.

4
Absorption and reflection of sound energy

In the discussion of travelling waves some reference has been made to the frequency of the sound vibrations but none has been made to the amplitude of the waves. Whatever frequency or indeed mixture of frequencies is generated by the sound source will be present in the sound-waves propagated in the surrounding air. The amplitude of the waves is, however, subject to a number of factors which will be discussed in the course of this chapter. The key to the matter lies in the amount of energy which is available for conversion into sound. The amplitude of vibration of the tuning-fork prong is largely determined by the strength of the blow with which we strike it; this decides the total energy that is injected into the vibrating system. The fork goes on vibrating until this energy is used up and then it ceases to move. Part of the energy is consumed in moving repeatedly the metal particles of the fork; part of it is expended in moving the air particles around the prong and in imparting energy to them. If the foot of the fork is pressed on a bench top, for example, then some of the energy is used in moving the bench on which the foot of the fork is placed, and this in turn moves the surrounding air particles. The point is simply that all the energy imparted to the fork is used up in some way; none of it is 'lost'. This same principle applies to all instances of vibration and sound; in the case of travelling waves, some of the ways in which energy is used up are rather more complex.

Let us go back for a moment to the example of the rope tied at one end to a post. A movement of the hand will impart a wave-motion to the stretched rope which will travel towards the post. The total energy available will depend on the force used and the distance through which the hand travels. The energy will be used up in moving the rope particles and imposing the wave-motion on them; it will in fact determine the amplitude of this motion. If the rope is long or if little force is applied, the wave-motion will persist for only the first few metres of the rope and the

37

amplitude will die down rapidly, rather like that of the damped wave shown in Fig. 13. If the rope is short and a great deal of force is applied, the wave-motion will travel as far as the post. Let us look closely at what happens at this point. We will imagine the rope particles to be rather in the nature of slices of rope, with the last slice firmly fixed to the post, and the phase of the motion to be such that the adjacent slices have just been made to skip up in the air, that is they are in the positive half of the cycle of movement. This means that the energy transferred to the fixed slice will make a feeble attempt to pull the post out of the ground. It will not of course succeed and the result will be that the wave-motion will begin to travel back along the rope, in other words there will be *reflection* of the wave-motion. The reflected wave will travel onwards as long as there is any of the original store of energy left to move the rope particles and the amplitude of the wave will die down as the energy is used up.

The wave-motion in the rope provides an example in which reflection is visible but something exactly analogous occurs with sound waves. When sounds travel outwards from a sound source, the waves encounter all kinds of obstacles and in certain conditions, which we shall look into a little later, they may be reflected from these obstacles. The echoes which can be heard coming back from a hillside, a wood or a building are instances of sound reflection. A short-lived sound such as a shouted word or a handclap will travel outwards from the source and reach, perhaps, a distant hillside; there the sound waves will be reflected and after an interval arrive back at our ears. If there are several such obstacles in the path of the sound, we may hear two or three echoes, which will arrive back at different times because the obstacles are at different distances and the sounds have to travel there and back at the standard speed of 340 m/s. In every case the echo is much fainter than the original sound, which means that the amplitude of the returning wave is less than that of the wave generated at the sound source. This is inevitable since the sum of energy available is limited and is being used up in moving air particles between the source and the hill and also incidentally in trying to shift the hill itself, just as the rope tried to pull the post out of the ground.

We generally use the word 'echo' in cases where there is a time interval between the outgoing and the returning sound. The same phenomenon of reflection occurs in ordinary rooms and in concert halls where distances are comparatively short and there is usually overlap between the outgoing and the reflected sound; in this case we refer to it as *reverberation* but the physical principle involved is the same. If the sound produced is short enough, a true echo can be heard in a concert hall and this is why acoustic tests of such buildings often include the firing of a pistol shot, for this allows measurement of the reflected sound unmixed with the outgoing sound. The amount of reverberation present in a room or any enclosed space can be modified in a number of ways. An ordinary living room which has been emptied of furniture is much more reverberant than the same room furnished; a lecture or concert hall full of people is less reverberant than the same hall when empty. It is clear that furniture and people must be soaking up or absorbing sound energy, leaving much less of it to be returned in the form of reflected sound waves.

The *absorption* or *reflection* of sound energy is not an all-or-none business; it is very much influenced by the relation between the wavelength of a given sound and the size of the obstacle which it meets. Broadly speaking, a sound wave will be reflected if the obstacle or surface it meets is somewhat larger than its wavelength and will tend to be absorbed if it is smaller. This accounts in part for the materials used in acoustic treatment of rooms, the object of which is generally sound absorption; perforated panels, rough textured and porous surfaces and hangings present effectively many small obstacles to the sound waves and also increase the actual area interposed in their path and they thus provide sound absorption over a wide range of frequencies.

Standing waves

We will now examine a particular case of sound reflection which has some important acoustic implications. Imagine a perfectly bare room, 4 m long, with very smooth and rigid wall surfaces. In the middle of the room we set strongly into vibration a tuning fork of frequency 515 cycles. Sound waves travel out in all directions from the fork but in order to simplify matters we will consider only a small part of the horizontal path from the fork to the end walls. Since the frequency of vibration is 515 c.p.s., the wavelength must be 340/515 m which is 66 cm. Allowing a short distance in the middle of the room for the vibrating fork, there will be just room to right and left of the fork for three complete wavelengths of the sound. At each wall conditions are very favourable to reflection and hence there will be a reflected wave whose amplitude is not very different from that of the original wave. The wavelength of the reflected wave is the same as that of the outgoing wave, so that again there will be just room for three wavelengths between each end wall and the fork. In Fig. 19 we see represented a segment of the outgoing and the reflected wave, which are

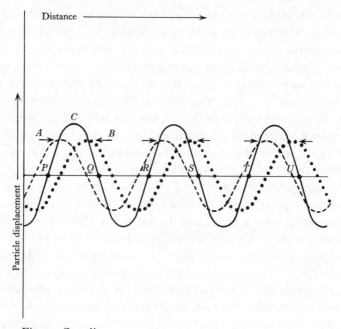

Fig. 19. Standing wave pattern.

moving through space in opposite directions: wave *A* is moving to the right and wave *B* to the left. The effect of these two wave-motions will be added together algebraically, in the manner that is explained on p. 21, and the result will be the wave shown as a continuous curve, wave *C*. There are six points in space where this curve passes through zero because here the waves *A* and *B* are exactly in opposite phase, that is to say that *A* has a positive value exactly equal to the negative value of *B*, as at the point labelled *P*, or vice versa, as at point *Q*. This figure represents the state of affairs at just one instant, and remember that the waves are travelling. Imagine the position a few tenths of a millisecond later; wave *A* will have moved a short distance to the right and wave *B* an equal distance to the left, let us suppose that they now coincide with the former wave *C*. The amplitude of *C* will now be greater, equal to twice the positive value of *A* (or *B*). Notice however that the resultant wave *C* will still have zeros at the same points in space as before, those labelled *P*, *Q*, *R*, *S*, *T*, *U*. Waves *A* and *B* are changing their relations at every moment, but no matter how these relations change, the zeros of the resultant wave are always at the same points. This means literally that at these points the air particles do

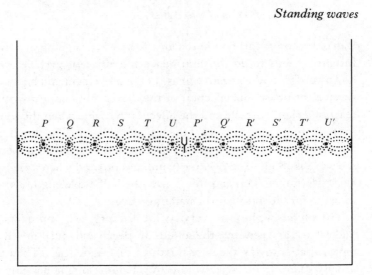

Fig. 20. Standing waves in a room.

not move because they are being subjected to equal and opposite forces by wave *A* and wave *B*. At all other points the air particles are on the move through varying distances as the forces of waves *A* and *B* add together and subtract. A very simplified impression of this effect is given by Fig. 20. The points at which there is no particle motion are called *nodes*; they occur at spatial intervals of a half-wavelength and therefore in our example there are six nodes to the right of the tuning fork and six to the left. Between the nodes there are points where particles attain the maximum of displacement and these are called *antinodes*. Because nodes impose a fixed pattern on the wave-motions, such waves are called *standing waves*. In Figs. 19 and 20 the waves are represented as though they were transverse waves; this is done simply to make the presentation clearer; the actual sound waves are of course longitudinal waves which obey the same laws.

The wave-motion we have been looking at is but one of many that result from the movement of the tuning fork, since it is sending out sound waves in all directions. Provided there is reflection of the sound, there will be standing waves along any path which measures an exact multiple of the half-wavelength of the sound. There will thus be a large number of nodes in the whole air space of the room. In the situation illustrated by Fig. 20, the reflected wave is in opposite phase to the outgoing wave. It is easier to appreciate why this should be so, perhaps, from the example of the stretched rope. When the wave-motion reaches the fixed end of the rope, it may try to lift this end in the air, if the wave is going positive at that instant. It fails to do this and hence the adjacent particles are forced downwards into the negative phase of the movement and hence there is a reversal of phase on reflection of the wave. This occurs when a wave reaches a rigid obstacle and the effect is the same when the sound wave from the tuning fork arrives at the wall of the room. The standing wave is not disturbed by this change of phase because a node occurs both when the wave is about to go positive (compression) and when it is about to go negative (rarefaction) and this is why the half-wavelength is the critical measure for the setting up of standing waves.

The sounds we hear in everyday life are very rarely pure tones, as was said earlier, and certainly the sounds of speech and music are all complex tones, that is to say they are mixtures of frequencies. Thus there are usually many frequencies whose wavelengths might possibly fall into standing wave patterns. A marked degree of sound reflection is a prerequisite for this and one purpose of acoustic treatment of rooms and halls for public performance is the avoidance of such patterns. At the same time a hall in which there is very little reverberance, that is reflection, is unsatisfactory because it makes everything sound 'dead' and rather unpleasant. The objective generally is to strike a balance between too much and too little reverberation. In theatres and halls where there happen to be 'dead' spots, the probability is that at these places nodes are rather readily established for quite a range of frequencies so that anyone sitting in that position receives little sound energy from the stage or platform.

Modes of vibration

The reflection of wave-motions may take place in any medium in which they occur. If enough energy were imparted to waves on the surface of a pond, they might travel as far as the edge of the pond and they would there be reflected and begin to travel back again; we have seen too that the wave-motion in a stretched rope can be reflected from its fixed end just as sound waves are reflected from the wall of a room. The reflection of wave-motions in solids and gases is an important factor in the generation of sounds, particularly those of music. A large proportion of the instruments in an orchestra are stringed instruments and a consideration of the principles of sound generation by means of a stretched string forms a good starting point for the present discussion.

Quite a variety of instruments depend upon the stretched string for the production of tone and they differ from each other mainly in their size and in the method of setting the string into vibration, that is of applying force. The violin, viola, 'cello and double-bass are usually bowed, though they may be plucked, the guitar, the harp and the harpsichord are plucked, and in the piano, which must be included in this class, the strings are struck with hammers. In every case the vibrating element is a length of string stretched between two fixed points. The violin string, which may be taken as typical, runs from a tuning peg at the scroll end of the instrument, passes over the nut, a small grooved bridge at the end of the finger-board and at the other end over the bridge of the violin. Because of the tension on the string, the points at the bridge and the nut are fixed and only the length of string in between is free to vibrate when bowed or plucked. By either of these means the string is drawn aside from its position of rest and when released it goes into vibration. The wave-motion in the string is in fact transverse and not longitudinal. The vibratory movement travels along the string in both directions from the point where it is displaced, and at each end encounters a fixed point. The wave is therefore reflected from these points and standing waves are set up with a node at each end of the string. From the earlier discussion of standing waves we know that adjacent nodes are separated by a half-wavelength, so that the frequency of the note given out by the string will be equivalent to a wavelength twice the length of the string. We must remember of course that wavelength is dependent on velocity of propagation and we are here talking about wave-motion in catgut, if that is the material of the string, so it would be a mistake to base calculations on wavelengths in air. Furthermore, the frequency of the note given out is not dependent solely on the length of the string, as is quite obvious from the fact that the four strings of the violin are the same length yet each is tuned to a different frequency.

When playing, the violin player puts his fingers down on the strings, thereby altering the effective length of the string. One fixed point is still at the bridge but the other is not now at the nut; it is wherever the finger is pressed down on the string. The distance between adjacent nodes is shortened, the half-wavelength is less and hence the frequency must be higher. In playing a scale on one string, for example, the violinist moves his fingers progressively up the string towards the bridge. By means of this technique of 'stopping' the string with the fingers and by using all four strings of the instrument, the player is able to cover a very wide range of frequencies; in the case of the violin, the notes cover a pitch range of over three octaves. The same principles are used in the viola, 'cello, double-bass and guitar. In the piano, the harp and the harpsichord there are strings of differing length for all the notes produced.

In discussing the occurrence of standing waves in a room we noted that for a given dimension of the room there would be many frequencies whose half-wavelength would fit an exact number of times into the distance between the source and the wall. The same thing holds for a stretched string and in fact when such a string is set vibrating, many different standing waves occur in the course of its motion. We must bear in mind that an essential requirement is that such standing waves fit exactly into the length of the string, that is to say that each must have nodes at the bridge and at the nut (if we consider the open string, that is not stopped by a finger). The pattern for several standing waves which satisfy the requirement is shown in Fig. 21. Example *A* is the wave involving the whole length of the string, with a node at each end only. In *B* there is an additional node at the mid-point of the string, so that it is vibrating in two halves; in *C* there are four nodes altogether and the string is vibrating in segments of a third, while in *D* and *E* it is vibrating in quarters and fifths respectively. The curves in the figure are simply a diagrammatic representation of the different positions occupied by the particles of the string as time passes. The motion of the string is so complex that it is impossible to visualize the shape of the vibrating string at any given instant. These are transverse waves and each particle of the string is being displaced vertically by forces corresponding to a combination of the curves in the figure. Each standing wave pattern is referred to as a *mode of vibration*, so the string is vibrating simultaneously in a number of different modes, that is over its whole length, in halves, in thirds, etc.

The principle can perhaps be made a little clearer by noting that there are ways in which certain modes of vibration in the string may be prevented. String players and also harpists often have to play 'harmonics'. The violinist does this, for example, by placing a finger tip lightly on the middle point of a string, and bowing the string. The effect of this is to impose a node at the mid-point of the string and this means that the string can no longer vibrate in any mode which requires motion of the string particles at that point. The mode of vibration denoted in Fig. 21 *A* will be suppressed; *B* and *D* will still be possible because they require a node in the middle of the string but *C* and *E* will also be suppressed. This leads us to the most important implication of different

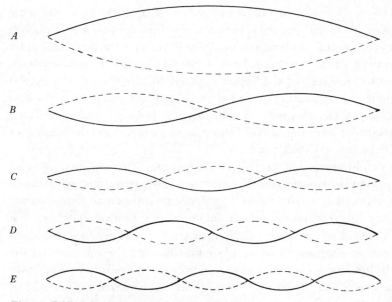

Fig. 21. Different modes of vibration in a string.

modes of vibration, which lies in the relation between the vibratory
movement and the frequency of the sound which is produced.

In the first mode of vibration, over the whole length of the string, the
string length determines the half-wavelength of the sound. With the
string vibrating in halves, the half-wavelength must clearly be halved
which means that the frequency of the sound is doubled. In *C*, *D* and *E*
the half-wavelength is respectively one third, one quarter and one fifth of
A and hence the frequency is multiplied by 3, by 4 and by 5. If the sound
given out by mode *A* were 100 c.p.s. (the string would have to be a 'cello
string rather than a violin string), then the other modes would produce
frequencies of 200, 300, 400 and 500 c.p.s. respectively. Such a series of
frequencies has great importance from the acoustic point of view. The
sequence of numbers is known as a *harmonic series*; the mode of vibration
involving the whole length of the string is called the *fundamental mode*
and the frequency to which it gives rise is the *fundamental frequency*. The
frequencies produced by the other modes are the *harmonics* and these are
numbered consecutively upwards, the one above the fundamental being
called the *second harmonic*, and so on. In our example, the fundamental
frequency is 100 c.p.s., the second harmonic is 200 c.p.s., the third, 300

and so on. Numbers in a harmonic series are obtained by taking some number as the starting point (acoustically this is always the frequency produced by the fundamental mode) and multiplying this number by successive whole numbers. Thus if the fundamental frequency were raised to 120 c.p.s., by the 'cellist's putting his finger on the string, for example, the frequencies of the harmonics would now be 120 multiplied by 2, 3, 4, 5, etc., that is to say 240, 360, 480, 600 c.p.s. and so on. If the fundamental were raised still further to 150 c.p.s., then the harmonics would be 300, 450, 600, 750 c.p.s.

It should be stressed that this is not a theoretical or mathematical point but a matter of acoustic fact. The vibrating violin string does not produce a pure tone, that is a sine wave; it produces a complex tone consisting of a mixture of frequencies which includes the fundamental and the harmonics. Each mode of vibration by itself would produce sinusoidal motion but they are all taking place together and the waveform of the resulting sound is a complex wave, which can be arrived at by the addition of the sine waves; this is the reason for dealing with this technique in an earlier chapter. In the example shown in Fig. 21, we have illustrated modes only up to the fifth harmonic. In practice, a violin note may include harmonics higher than this, up to the eighth or even the tenth, so that the waveform would be more complex than that obtained by the addition of these five sine waves.

The example of the vibrating string offers the clearest approach to the subject of modes of vibration and this class of wave-motion plays a major role in music. Its chief importance for us, however, is as an analogy for the wave-motions which take place in columns of air, for it is this type of vibration which lies behind the operation of the speech mechanism as well as forming the basis of a whole range of musical sounds. All the wind instruments of the orchestra, both brass and woodwind, produce their music by setting into motion a column of air. We may take the oboe as a typical example. The body of the instrument is a wooden tube which encloses a column of air. There are holes in the wooden tube which can be closed by the action of keys and the function of these is to alter the effective length of the tube, just as the violinist changes the effective length of his string by pressing his finger down on the finger-board. The oboe has a mouthpiece with a double reed which the player holds in his mouth, and this obviously closes the tube at the upper end. The lower end is open to the outer air. When all the keys of the instrument are closed, the column of air contained in the oboe extends from the mouth of the player to the open bell of the instrument. While it is easy to see that there will be reflections from the upper end of the column, which is closed, and that this point will form a node for standing waves, it is more difficult to understand that there are reflections from the open end of the tube; at this stage it is best simply to accept as a physical fact that such reflections do take place and that there are standing waves in the column of air. It is intuitively more readily acceptable that the open end does not constitute a node but an antinode, that is a place where there is maximum displacement of the particles. By referring to Fig. 21 we can see that the distance from a node to the next antinode is equal to a quarter-wavelength of the vibration and hence the total length of the air column gives a quarter of the wavelength of the frequency generated in the fundamental mode. Frequencies generated by other modes of vibration are multiples of this frequency.

The wave-motions set up in a column of air, unlike those in a vibrating string, are longitudinal waves, but in other respects the two methods of producing sound are analogous. Reflections occur in the vibrating air column and give rise to standing waves; there is a series of modes of vibration, each generating a different frequency but with all frequencies related by being members of the same harmonic series, composed of a fundamental frequency and harmonics which are exact multiples of the fundamental. The total sound output of the system is therefore a mixture of frequencies, a complex tone, of which the waveform can be arrived at by the addition of the component sine waves, provided that the amplitude and phase of these is known.

The factors which determine the amplitude of the harmonics in a frequency mixture are very complex and we shall examine some of them in the next chapter. We noted, for example, the suppressing of a range of harmonic frequencies on a stringed instrument by imposing a node, as the violinist does when he plays a 'harmonic'. Analogous effects are produced by imposing an antinode. If a string is plucked just at the mid-point, for example, this creates an antinode, a maximum of displacement, so that any harmonic requiring a node at this place is suppressed. The bowing of a stringed instrument takes place at roughly one-seventh of the length of the string, thus reducing if not entirely suppressing the seventh harmonic of the fundamental, which is musically dissonant or discordant. In the piano the strings are struck by the hammers at about the same relative position, with similar effect. Suppressing a harmonic means that it is reduced to zero amplitude. Apart from such special effects, harmonics in a mixture will have differing amplitudes, with a tendency for the amplitude to decrease as the number of the harmonic rises.

Sound quality

In a previous chapter we noted that the frequency of a sound is chiefly responsible for the pitch that we hear and amplitude for the loudness. The harmonic structure of a sound, that is the relative amplitudes of the fundamental and the harmonics, is important because it is the principal determinant of sound quality. It is quite possible for two sounds to be of the same pitch and of the same loudness and yet to be very different from each other in quality; when this happens, there is certainly a difference in the arrangement of the amplitudes of the harmonics, although in both cases they are based on the same fundamental frequency. When the orchestra tunes to the A given out by the oboe, many different kinds of instrument are producing notes of the same pitch and we identify the various instruments because of the differences in the harmonic structure of the sounds. The sound of the flute, for example, is characterized by high amplitude of the fundamental and the second harmonic, with very little energy in any of the higher harmonics, and this accounts for the rounded quality which we hear when the flute plays. In the oboe, on the other hand, a whole range of higher harmonics, from the fourth up to the tenth or twelfth, show considerable amplitude and they explain the acute, 'squeaky' tone which we associate with this instrument. The clarinet too has some higher harmonics but they are in a much narrower range than the oboe's, and the fundamental is relatively much stronger. The sound of a tuning fork is quite without character simply because the fork has only one mode of vibration, the fundamental mode, and all the harmonics have zero amplitude. Such differences as these are the basis for our perception of differences in sound quality; we shall see later on that the same principle lies behind many of the perceptual differences between speech sounds.

5
Free and forced vibrations: resonance

Up to this point we have concerned ourselves only with sounds which result from applying a force to some vibrating system and then removing the source of energy, leaving the system as it were to its own devices. This is the situation when we strike the tuning fork or hit the table top, pluck a string or strike a piano key; we supply force once and the system emits a sound whose characteristics are determined by its own properties. It may last for a long time, as it does in the case of the tuning fork, or die almost immediately, as in the case of the table top; it may be the result of many modes of vibration, as in the plucked string and the piano, or of a single mode, as in the tuning fork, and this means that it is either a complex tone consisting of a fundamental frequency and an extended range of harmonics or a pure tone. All wave-motions that are produced in this way, by applying a force for a very brief time and then removing it, are the result of *free vibrations*. A system which is performing free vibrations will be oscillating at its *natural frequency*, and this term refers to the fundamental frequency, since any harmonics that are generated will be tied to this frequency.

In the generation of sound waves there are, however, other possibilities which another familiar example will help to make clear. A tuning fork which has been struck will give out a sound which we can hear if we hold the fork close to the ear but which is certainly not audible very far away. If we want to make it so, we simply press the foot of the fork on a table top and the sound is considerably louder. This is because the table top is now vibrating, as well as the fork, and it is quite clear that it cannot be performing free vibrations. When we hit the table top it gives out a dull sound of no particular pitch which dies out almost immediately. This sound is the result of free vibrations of the table top and it is very different from what we hear when the tuning fork is vibrating. Let us see exactly what is happening in this case, with the help of Fig. 22. The prongs of the

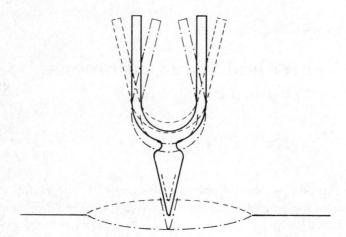

Fig. 22. Forced vibration in response to a tuning fork.

tuning fork move away from each other and towards each other in each cycle of movement. They are continuous with the foot of the fork, so that when the prongs are wide apart, the foot must rise in the air a little, and when they are closer together, the foot must descend. The foot of the fork is now pressed onto the table top and hence the up-and-down motion is conveyed to the table, or at least a portion of the top surface. The foot has no choice but to move exactly in time with the prongs and the table top must move exactly in time with the foot of the fork, so that its movement has the same frequency as that of the fork. The fork is now coupled to the table top and the latter is performing *forced vibrations*.

In the case of free vibrations a force is applied and the source is then withdrawn; in forced vibrations force is applied repeatedly so that energy is continually being supplied to the system which is being forced into vibration. We can think of the energy supply as being the *driving force*; the system to which it is applied is the *driven system*. In our example, the tuning fork supplies the driving force and it is the table top which is being driven. The first point to notice is that forced vibrations are at the frequency of the driving force. Let us suppose that our tuning fork is giving out the note middle C, with a frequency of 264 Hz, then the forced vibrations of the table top will have the same frequency.* If we change the tuning fork to one which gives out the orchestral A, 440 Hz, then we shall

* From this point onwards the commonly used abbreviation Hz replaces c.p.s. to denote cycles per second.

hear this note coming from the table top; the forced vibrations will now have a frequency of 440 Hz.

In out initial discussion of sound generation and also of sound propagation we have simplified the picture in order not to anticipate the subject of forced vibrations; we have in fact dealt with a number of examples in which the principle is involved. If we consider the case of a vibrating tuning fork simply held in the hand, we know that the motion of the fork will send out sound waves into the air; the air particles are being forced into vibration for they do not perform free vibrations at audible frequencies. If they did, then the air particles would 'ring' every time you waved your hand, and we know that they do not.

Forced vibrations arise because the driving force is coupled to, that is connected with, the driven system, and the coupling may be more or less efficient. The layers of air next to the prongs of the vibrating tuning fork are coupled with its motion by mere juxtaposition. When the foot of the fork is pressed on the table top, we hear a louder sound which is due to a combination of two effects. The coupling of the foot of the fork to the table top is rather more effective than the coupling of the prongs to the air and in addition a considerable area of the table is set into motion; this area in turn is in contact with air particles and thus forms an additional source of sound waves. What we hear is therefore the sum of the sound waves generated by the prongs of the fork in the surrounding air plus those arising from the air which is in contact with the moving table top.

Amplitude of forced vibrations

It is clear from this example that the amplitude of the forced vibrations set up by a given driving force will depend in part on how tightly the two elements are coupled together. This can be checked easily enough with a tuning fork if the fork is set vibrating and the foot is first lightly touched on a table top and then pressed down; the sound is noticeably louder when the foot is pressed down. There is another factor, however, which is much more important and which is concerned with the relations between the natural frequencies of the driven system and the driving force.

Imagine that we set up two tuning forks each with a natural frequency of 100 Hz. We are going to use one as a driving force and the second as a driven system. In order to couple them together we solder one end of a metal rod to the right-hand prong of fork A and the other end to the left-hand prong of fork B, the arrangement shown in Fig. 23. Fork A is going

Fork *A*   Fork *B*

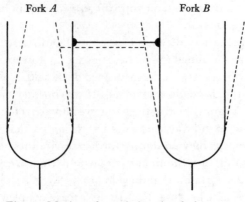

Fig. 23. Motion of coupled tuning forks.

to act as the driving force, so we give it a strong blow to set it vibrating. The first thing that happens is that the prongs of fork *A* move towards each other and since the right prong is rigidly connected to the left prong of fork *B*, the prongs of the latter are obliged to move outwards. Fork *A* carries out its cycle of movement repeatedly, reversing direction at each half-cycle (that is every 5 ms) and fork *B* is forced to follow its movement. But the natural frequency of fork *B* is 100 Hz; if it were not coupled to fork *A* and we think of the very first impulse it has received as being a light tap which sets it vibrating, then it would be performing the same motion, reversing direction every 5 ms.

Supposing now that we replace fork *B* by another whose natural frequency is 125 Hz and we couple it to fork *A* in the same way. The first impulse from fork *A* sets it moving but after 4 ms the new fork tries to reverse direction because this fits in with its natural frequency of 125 Hz, and it is therefore now opposing the driving force. After the first 5 ms fork *A* reverses direction and for a few milliseconds the natural tendency of the new fork is in line with the driving force, but after 8 ms it will again wish to reverse its direction. For a proportion of successive cycles, therefore, the driven system will be opposing the driving force. The second fork has no choice but to follow the motion of fork *A*, because of the rigid coupling between the forks, but the effect of this opposition is greatly to reduce the amplitude of the forced vibrations.

We will now return to the example of the table top which can be forced into vibration also by a tuning fork. A single blow on the table top will produce its free vibrations which might well be of a frequency of 100 Hz.

If we press the foot of a 100 Hz fork which is vibrating on the table, we shall produce forced vibrations of some amplitude, since the natural tendency of the table top is to keep in step with and not to oppose the driving force at any moment. The table top has a further property, however, and that is that it is highly damped; when it performs free vibrations, they are likely to have the kind of waveform illustrated in Fig. 13. As a consequence any force imported to the table top will be rapidly used up so that there will be little tendency for it to oppose a driving force applied to it, even if the frequency is different from its own natural frequency; in this respect it has very little will of its own. This is a matter of practical experience, since a tuning fork of almost any frequency placed on any table will evoke a noticeable response. It is still the case, of course, that the greatest amplitude of forced vibrations is obtained from the table top by a driving force which coincides with its natural frequency.

Forced vibrations are not confined to things like table tops and tuning forks; anything which will vibrate can, in the right conditions, be made to perform forced vibrations. From the point of view of speech, the most important fact is that columns of air can be forced to vibrate. This can be demonstrated fairly simply by using a tuning fork and a reasonably narrow glass jar, like the gas jars used in chemistry laboratories. If the fork is set vibrating strongly and held over the mouth of the jar, there may or may not be some audible response. While the fork is vibrating, pour water slowly and gently into the jar and as the water level rises you will probably reach a moment when the sound of the fork rings out loudly and clearly from the jar. This is because the column of air is now of the right length to have a natural frequency coincident with that of the fork and it therefore performs forced vibrations of considerable amplitude.

Here we have begun with a driving force of a certain frequency and have varied the driven system in such a way as to get the maximum amplitude of forced vibrations. We could work in the reverse direction, using a fixed system, for example the glass jar without any water, and varying the frequency of the driving force to see how the system reacts. This would call for a large supply of tuning forks and is done much more conveniently by replacing the tuning fork by a small loudspeaker and an oscillator which gives out a whole range of pure tones. By employing a sound-level meter, which registers the amplitude of the sound given out by the system, we can draw a graph of the kind shown in Fig. 24 which relates the amplitude of forced vibrations with the frequency of the driving force. The natural frequency of the air column in the glass jar is

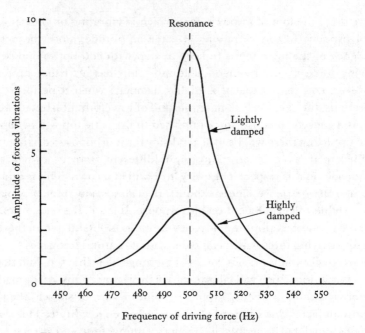

Fig. 24. Resonance curves for lightly damped and highly damped systems.

500 Hz and, as we have already established, the maximum amplitude of forced vibrations is obtained when the driving force has this frequency. In the figure, the frequency of the driving force is shown on the horizontal scale in hertz and the amplitude of the forced vibrations is given in arbitrary units on the vertical scale. As the frequency of the driving force departs from the natural frequency of the driven system, the amplitude of the forced vibrations decreases and it does so symmetrically, that is the amplitudes are equal at 510 Hz and at 490 Hz and so on. The condition in which the frequency of the driving force is the same as the natural frequency of the driven system is the condition of *resonance*. It should be noticed that this is the technical meaning of the term, although it is used more loosely in many contexts. The kind of curve which relates the frequency of the driving force with the amplitude of forced vibrations is called a *resonance curve*; Fig. 24 shows two examples, one for a system which is lightly damped and the other for a more highly damped system.

An increase in damping has two effects on the resonance curve: it makes the curve less sharply peaked and it reduces the general level of amplitude that is recorded for the forced vibrations. This is understandable since, as we saw in Chapter 2, damping is the property which causes a system to soak up energy in overcoming frictional forces, thus reducing the amount of energy converted into vibratory movement. An analogy may help to make this clearer. If you walk through water which comes up to your ankles, you feel a certain resistance which you have to overcome in order to make progress; if the water is up to your knees, movement becomes much more difficult and if it is up to your thighs, you have to put out a great deal of energy to make any movement at all. It is not a mere punning observation that in this case the damping has been progressively increased. In vibrating systems a high degree of damping means that this resistance to movement is relatively great and there is little oscillation for a given force applied to the system; this is true of course for both free and forced vibrations. We have already seen in the example of the table top that a high degree of damping also means that the system is relatively indifferent to the frequency of the driving force and therefore the resonance curve is flatter. The two curves of Fig. 24 might refer on the one hand to the glass jar and the air column within it (lightly damped) and the table top (highly damped) on the other. In the case of the glass jar, the degree of damping could be altered, for example by spreading some cotton wool in the jar; this could increase the damping without shifting the point of resonance and give a curve between the two shown in the figure.

We can now bring together several characteristics of resonating systems. Whatever the properties of the system, the greatest amplitude of forced vibrations will occur where the condition of resonance is attained, that is where the frequency of the driving force coincides with the natural frequency of the driven system; in this condition we get the greatest output for a given input of energy. A system which is lightly damped, when it is performing free vibrations will give a high return for a given input of energy and in particular will go on vibrating or 'ringing' for a long time; when it is performing forced vibrations, it will again give a high output in the form of high-amplitude forced vibrations, but it will be very selective as to the frequency of the driving force, and will give very little response when this frequency departs very far from the condition of resonance; it will have a narrow, sharp peak to the resonance curve. Because of this selectivity, such a system is said to be *sharply tuned*. The vibrations of a system which is highly damped die away very rapidly when they are free vibrations, and have relatively little amplitude when they are forced vibrations; it will, however, respond to a much wider range of driving frequencies, it is not sharply tuned and has a flat resonance curve.

Complex tones and forced vibrations

In the discussion of forced vibrations so far we have referred only to the 'frequency' of the driving force and the examples have involved the use of a tuning fork which does indeed give out a single frequency. But practically all the sounds we hear are complex tones and the systems which generate them are sending out a mixture of frequencies, so that in real situations the driving force is almost certain to contain more than one frequency and probably a whole range of harmonics. What happens when the driving force contains a number of frequencies? The principle remains quite unchanged; if we are driving a given system, such as the air column in the glass jar, its behaviour will be as before and if the complex of frequencies which constitutes the driving force includes the natural frequency of the system, then the condition of resonance will obtain and there will be a peak of output from the glass jar. The resonator as it were selects from the frequency mixture the particular frequency to which it responds.

In discussing orchestral wind instruments earlier we provided a very simplified view of their operation; they in fact depend upon the phenomenon which has just been outlined. The mouthpiece of an oboe or clarinet, if it is separated from the body of the instrument and blown through, emits a very loud squeak. This sound consists of a very wide range of frequencies. When the mouthpiece is coupled to the body of the oboe, for example, the latter acts as a resonator and selects from the range of frequencies the appropriate one for the note which is to be played. The resonator is adjustable because the length of the column of air is varied by the opening and closing of the keys, just as the column of air in the glass jar can be modified by pouring in water.

One further complication must be added to complete this account of forced vibrations. When discussing standing waves we saw that the body of the oboe has a number of modes of vibration which are related to the wavelengths of a range of harmonics. Since resonance depends upon a coincidence of frequencies, it must of course imply a coincidence of wavelengths and therefore a resonator like the body of the oboe will exhibit more than one resonance; any frequency which fits in with its various modes of vibration will evoke a resonance. The column of air in the glass jar, in our example, showed a resonance at 500 Hz. If we were to continue

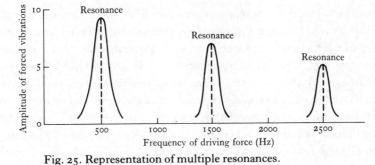

Fig. 25. Representation of multiple resonances.

to raise the frequency of the driving force well above this figure, we should discover that the glass jar has other resonances which appear at 1500 Hz and at 2500 Hz. The amplitude of the forced vibrations will decrease as the driving force gets higher and the resonance curves would probably be similar to those shown in Fig. 25. As we shall see in a later chapter, the principle of multiple resonances in a column of air is the basis of communication by speech. What it means is that if an air column is driven by a force which is rich in harmonics, the resonances of the air column will modify the amplitudes of the driving force so that the highest amplitudes in the resulting sound will be those of frequencies at which the column resonates.

Filters

The word resonance is used in so many contexts and so regularly with the implication that it is a 'good thing', that the idea inevitably arises that it affords some acoustic advantage. It must be kept in mind, however, that forced vibrations use up energy; a proportion of the driving force is spent in moving the resonating system and the balance may be given out as sound waves, but you cannot get more energy out of the whole operation than is put into it. Sounds can certainly be magnified but only by the use of such things as electronic amplifiers in which the additional energy required is provided in the form of electrical power. Resonators are not amplifiers and the energy they give out as sound waves is always less than the amount put into the system.

With this in mind, we can view the situation portrayed in Fig. 25 in two ways: the driven system will respond with high amplitude of forced vibrations to driving forces in the region of 500, 1500 and 2500 Hz, but equally it will absorb energy from forces in the range 600–1400 and

1600–2400 Hz. When resonators are considered more from the viewpoint of this second function they are often referred to as *filters*. The word has very much its everyday sense of an arrangement which will keep certain elements out, whether it be tobacco tars in the case of a cigarette or impurities in the case of water. Acoustic filters keep out or, more accurately, reduce the amplitude of certain ranges of frequency while allowing other frequency bands to pass with very little reduction of amplitude. The speech mechanism makes extensive use of this filtering function of resonators. In acoustic work it is often necessary to filter sounds artificially and this is accomplished by using electronic filters, that is circuits which are analogous to acoustic resonators, allowing the passage of signals in one frequency band and suppressing all others. One application of filters of this type will be touched upon in the following section.

Sound spectrum

Most of the sounds we hear and all of the sounds of speech are complex tones and a large proportion of them are frequency mixtures consisting of a fundamental frequency plus frequencies in the harmonic series. The description and specification of sounds therefore involves the statement of what frequencies are to be found in the mixture and what their relative amplitudes are. Such a statement is said to refer to the *spectrum* of the sound. This term is clearly borrowed from optics where the spectrum of light is given by the various wavelengths of which the light is composed. A sound spectrum is exactly analogous but is stated in terms of frequency instead of wavelength since sound travels through different media. To arrive at the spectrum of a sound we need to break it up into its component frequencies and to measure the relative amplitude of all the components; this information is obtained by the process of *acoustic analysis*. The results of the acoustic analysis of a sound could be presented in a table which stated that the fundamental frequency was, say, 100 Hz which had an amplitude of 8 units, the second harmonic, 200 Hz had an amplitude of 5 units, the third harmonic, 300 Hz had zero amplitude, and so on. When presented in a graphic form, however, the information is much more readily assimilated and in particular it becomes much easier to compare the spectra of different sounds, which is one of the main purposes of acoustic analysis.

One form in which sound spectra are often shown is illustrated in Fig. 26. Frequencies are set out on the horizontal scale in hertz. The relative

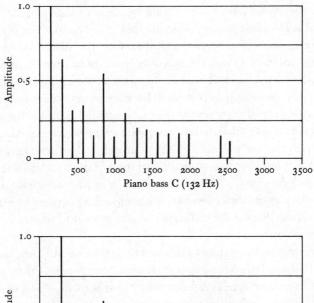

Piano bass C (132 Hz)

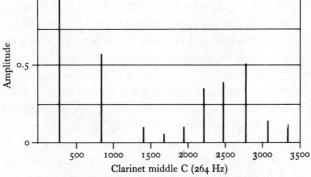

Clarinet middle C (264 Hz)

Fig. 26. Spectra of piano and clarinet tones.

amplitude of the components is given with reference to the vertical scale; the component with the greatest amplitude is given the value 1.0 and the amplitude of all other components is expressed as a proportion of this value. Wherever a vertical line is drawn, there is a component of that frequency present in the mixture with the amplitude indicated; at all other frequencies there is zero sound energy. The two examples are the bass C of the piano, one octave below middle C, with a fundamental frequency of 132 Hz and middle C played on the clarinet, fundamental 264 Hz. In each case any components represented in the spectrum must be in the harmonic series and consecutive harmonics will appear at an interval equal to the fundamental frequency. In the piano note consecutive harmonics occur over a wide frequency range and since the fundamental is low they appear close together. The fundamental of the clarinet note is an octave higher and therefore the distance between consecutive harmonics is doubled. It is only from about 1500 Hz upwards that consecutive harmonics appear in the clarinet tone; the second and fourth harmonics have zero amplitude. There are major differences in the mechanisms for generating sound in the piano and the clarinet: the piano tone is the result of free vibrations of the piano string which is struck by a hammer while the air column of the clarinet is performing forced vibrations in response to the continued vibration of the reed and does not show the rapid damping of the sound which is so characteristic of the piano. Nonetheless the differences in spectrum which appear in Fig. 26 are largely responsible for the difference in sound quality which we hear between the two instruments.

Differences in spectral pattern such as we see in this figure are usually recorded with the aid of a sound spectrograph, a device whose function is exactly what its name suggests, the drawing of a spectrum. The necessary acoustic analysis is done by means of electronic filters. The resonance curves of Fig. 25 could equally well represent the *response* of such filters tuned to 500, 1500 and 2500 Hz respectively. If a complex tone is fed into an analyser which includes these filters, then any component at 500 Hz or very close to it will be passed with very little loss by the filter and a measurement of the electrical output of the filter will give the relative amplitude of this component. Similarly the other two filters will register the amplitude of components in narrow bands centred on 1500 and 2500 Hz and of course the intervening frequency ranges can be explored in like manner to give a complete analysis of the sound. The patterns of Fig. 26 show one form that the resulting *spectrograms* may take and we shall see in later chapters that the spectrograph has proved an invaluable tool in the study of speech sounds.

6
The speech mechanism as sound generator

The acoustic principles formulated in the previous chapters provide a sufficient basis for a consideration of the acoustics of speech but, as we said earlier on, the sound waves of speech are among the most complex to be found in nature, particularly in the sense that extreme changes in sound quality follow each other with great rapidity. It follows from this that the speech mechanism viewed as a generator of sounds must work in a very complicated way and must indeed be capable of operating in a wide variety of ways. In this chapter we shall examine the basic properties of the speech mechanism in order to see what its principal modes of operation are and what kinds of sound they give rise to.

The musical instruments already used as examples consist essentially of a vibrating source of sound coupled to a resonating system and the speech mechanism is best considered in the same way. For a great deal of the time in speech the larynx is the *source* and the air column from the larynx to the lips, that is the *vocal tract* is the *system*. We know, however, that no sound can be produced without a supply of force or energy, so the first thing to establish is the nature of the energy supply for speech.

The energy supply in speech

Speech sounds may issue from a speaker in a continuous stream for quite an appreciable time and it is clear that the necessary force is not applied in one brief moment, as it is when a tuning fork is set in motion. It is the breathing mechanism, consisting of the lungs and the muscles of the chest and abdomen, that constitutes the energy supply. When we are not speaking, breathing is a rhythmical activity which involves taking air in and exhaling it on average about 15 times a minute, the actual rate depending upon the degree of physical activity. In quiet breathing the inspiratory and the expiratory phase of the cycle take about an equal time, so that if the cycle takes 4 seconds, 2 seconds is spent in breathing in and 2 seconds in breathing out. In speaking we use only the expiratory phase to supply energy and we change the waveform of the activity so that breathing in takes a very short time and expiration is spun out to occupy a much longer time, which in extreme cases may be 10–15 s.

Air flowing out from the lungs constitutes the force used in generating speech sounds, as it does indeed in the case of wind instruments which are producing musical sounds. In both cases, in order that sound shall be generated, the steady flow of energy in one direction has to be converted into to-and-fro movements or oscillations, first of some solid structures and then of air particles. In woodwind instruments the mechanism is the reed or reeds which form the mouthpiece; in brass instruments the player's lips are the vibrating elements. For speech the larynx performs this function, with the vocal cords acting rather like the lips of the brass player.

The larynx as sound source

By the use of the laryngeal muscles the vocal cords can be brought together so as to form as it were a shelf across the airway which leads from the lungs through the trachea to the pharynx and the mouth. The effect is illustrated in Fig. 27(*a*). There is a steady flow of air from the lungs into the trachea and while the edges of the cords are held together, pressure on the under side of the shelf rises. When it reaches a certain level, it is sufficient to overcome the resistance offered by the obstruction and so the vocal cords open approximately in the way shown in Fig. 27(*b*). The ligaments and muscle fibres that make up these structures have a degree of elasticity and having been forced out of position, they tend to return as rapidly as possible to their initial disposition and thus to obstruct the flow of air once more. The pressure rises again and the cycle of opening and closing is repeated so long as comparable conditions in the larynx are maintained. The return of the vocal cords to the closed position is not due solely to their elasticity; it is aided by a phenomenon which is known as the Bernoulli effect, after the scientist who first described the principle: the rapid increase in airflow when the cords open results in a drop in pressure and a consequent suction effect which tends to draw the cords back into the closed position.

Since air is being continuously expelled from the lungs, the alternate opening and closing of the vocal cords results in the emission of successive puffs of air into the space above the larynx and it is this stream of pulses which is the basis of the sound generated by the larynx. The

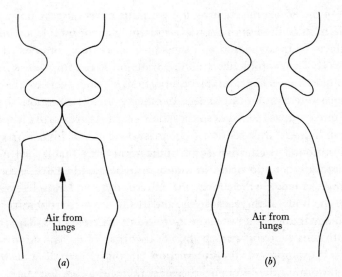

Fig. 27. Diagram of vocal fold motion.

time taken by one cycle of opening and closing of the cords depends upon the balance between the pressure below the cords, the *subglottal pressure*, and the resistance offered by the vocal folds, a convenient term for the ligaments and the muscles to which they are attached. This balance is under the control of the speaker and is the means by which we are able to change the frequency of vocal fold vibration at will.

Larynx frequency variation. The physical factors which regulate the frequency of vibration are the *mass, length* and *tension* of the vibrating structures, all of which are controlled by the intrinsic and extrinsic muscles of the larynx. The effect of these factors can be illustrated by the analogy of the stretched string, though it must be remembered that the vocal cords do not behave like strings. The strings which give out the low notes on a piano are obviously much longer and also much thicker and heavier than those which provide the top notes; it is clear that increasing the mass and increasing the length leads to a lower frequency of vibration. This is borne out by the orchestral stringed instruments, for the strings of the double-bass are longer and heavier than those of the violin. On the other hand, increasing the tension in a string raises the frequency of vibration; a string player sharpens the pitch of his string by screwing up a peg thus increasing the tension, and flattens the pitch by doing the opposite.

In the larynx mechanism, the vibrating parts can take on an infinity of different configurations and as a consequence the interaction between the effects of mass, length and tension is extremely complex. The closed phase of vocal fold vibration illustrated in Fig. 27(a) shows the folds in contact for a considerable proportion of their vertical height: they constitute a rather thick shelf. In other modes of vibration, the folds are thinned out at the edges so that the vibrating part is a great deal thinner and lighter; this reduction in mass leads to a higher frequency of vibration. The effective length of the vocal folds, that is the length which is actually set into vibratory motion, can be modified over a considerable range, chiefly by the action of the thyro-arytenoid muscles, which make up the body of the vocal folds, and of the crico-thyroid muscles, which change the angle between the thyroid and the cricoid cartilages and hence both lengthen and stretch the vocal cords. This last action provides a good example of the interaction of mass, length and tension in determining the frequency of vocal fold vibration. On the one hand it lengthens the cords and thus leads to a lowering of the frequency, but on the other hand it stretches the cords and this both increases the tension and thins the cords, both of which effects raise the frequency. For any 'setting' of the vocal folds, therefore, mass, length and tension are determined by muscle action and the fundamental mode of vibration is due to the resultant of the three factors.

The vocal folds have many modes of vibration in addition to the fundamental mode. Slow-motion pictures show for instance transverse waves travelling across the upper surface of the folds and when the contact between the two folds is extensive, as in Fig. 27(a), the opening of the folds begins at the bottom and travels upwards, so that there is a vertical wave-motion with a difference of phase between the opening of the lower and the upper surfaces. The wave generated by the whole larynx mechanism is therefore one of extreme complexity. The form of this wave has been arrived at by the use of several different techniques, principally by high-speed cinematography of the upper surface of the folds so as to register variations in the area between the edges of the two cords, and by measurement of variations in the airflow at the same place. The two methods give a wave which is substantially of the same general form, shown in Fig. 28. Time is represented on the horizontal axis and the vertical axis gives airflow in cubic centimetres per second. While the vocal cords are held in the closed position, no air is flowing at their upper surface and the corresponding part of the wave is a horizontal trace at the

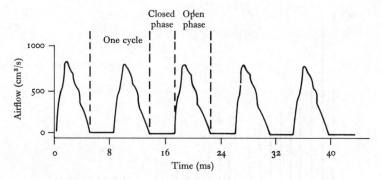

Fig. 28. Waveform of airflow at the larynx.

level of zero airflow. When the cords part, there is a rapid increase in airflow; the rise from zero to about 700 cm^3 takes just over 2 ms. As the cords begin to close together again, the airflow diminishes but at a somewhat slower rate, taking over 3 ms to return to zero, and it remains at zero for just over 3 ms before beginning the cycle again. The fundamental frequency is given by the time taken for one complete cycle; for the wave shown in Fig. 28 this is 8.3 ms, giving a frequency of 120 Hz.

The pitch of the larynx tone is determined by the frequency of the pulses emitted by the opening of the vocal cords; change in frequency means a change in the time occupied by one cycle, that is the closed phase plus the open phase. If the fundamental frequency were 100 Hz instead of 120 Hz, then the complete cycle of the glottal wave would take 10 ms; if it rose to 150 Hz, the time would be 6.7 ms and at 200 Hz it would be 5 ms.

The glottal wave is *periodic*, that is it consists of repeated cycles of motion, and therefore it must be made up of a fundamental frequency plus a range of harmonics. Consequently it must be possible to arrive at the waveform shown in Fig. 28 by adding sine waves together. The general shape of the wave is triangular and it may appear at first sight improbable that combining the curves we know as sine waves could ever result in such a shape. However, a sharp change in the direction of the wave implies simply that some event takes place in a very short time; given a sine wave of a high enough frequency, that is short enough wavelength, in the frequency mixture, sudden inflections can be produced in the complex wave. The quasi-triangular wave of Fig. 28 can be built up by adding an extended range of harmonic frequencies to the fundamental frequency so long as these harmonic components follow a

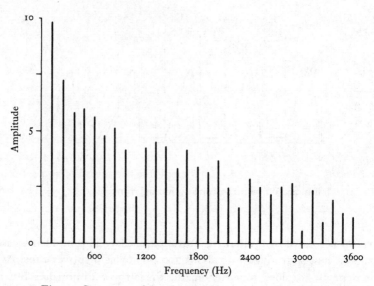

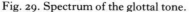

Fig. 29. Spectrum of the glottal tone.

certain general pattern of relative amplitude. The spectrum of Fig. 29 gives a good idea of what the amplitude pattern is for such a wave. Harmonics are shown up to a frequency of 3600 Hz, the 30th harmonic of 120 Hz, and the analysis has been stopped at this point; it does not mean that there is no energy at frequencies higher than this. The fundamental frequency has the greatest amplitude and each succeeding harmonic is represented, with the amplitude of harmonics falling off progressively as the frequency increases. This general trend is fairly regular but there are several dips in the spectrum indicating certain modes of vibration which have less amplitude than neighbouring ones.

The shape of the spectrum is not materially altered by a change of fundamental frequency but the spacing between the spectral lines is of course affected, as we saw in the case of the musical instruments. With a much higher pitch, such as might occur in a child's or woman's voice, the lines would be further apart and in a deep man's voice they might be closer together than those shown in the figure.

There are other features of the glottal wave which may vary, in addition to the fundamental frequency. The first is the overall or maximum amplitude of the wave. As we should expect, an increase in this amplitude will produce louder speech and a decrease, softer speech. The change is brought about mainly by increasing the general level of subglottal pressure through the action of the breathing muscles. A second feature is the ratio of the open phase to the closed phase in the cycle. In the wave shown in Fig. 28, the time occupied by the open phase is 0.6 of the total time of the cycle. The value for this factor varies with conditions and with individuals. With higher fundamental frequencies the open phase takes up a great proportion of the cycle; this is understandable since the period of the cycle becomes shorter. In individual speakers who speak in a breathy way, the closed phase may be very short or there may indeed be no complete closure during the cycle; the narrowing down of the space between the vocal cords is enough to generate the sound of voice, though the mechanism is not in this case working very efficiently. The most efficient method of phonation is to produce the maximum amplitude of wave for a given subglottal pressure and this is brought about by reducing the time of the open phase compared with the closed phase. This not only increases the overall amplitude of the wave but also increases the relative amplitude of the higher harmonics in the spectrum. What was said earlier about the role of high frequencies in forming a triangular wave is relevant here. A shorter open phase means that the triangle has a shorter base and a more acute angle at the apex, and the sides are nearer to the vertical. All this means that changes in the vibratory motion take place in a shorter time, that is generate higher frequencies.

Functions of larynx vibration in speech

Since the primary object of speech is communication between people, the first requirement of speech sounds is that they should be audible. The basic function of the sound source in the larynx is to make speech audible. The glottal wave whose characteristics we have been considering is as it were the carrier wave of speech, that is to say it does not itself contain a great deal of information but it acts as the vehicle by means of which information can be conveyed, just as the radio wave picked up by a radio receiver is the carrier for speech and music and many other kinds of sound. From this point of view larynx vibration is important because it provides us with the means of ensuring, in ordinary circumstances, that our speech is audible to listeners. We are nearly always surrounded by noise of some kind and we use our own ears in controlling the amplitude of our larynx vibrations so that our speech shall compete adequately with the noise.

Fundamental frequency. The fundamental frequency of vocal fold

67

vibration is one of the most important aspects of larynx activity as far as speech and language are concerned. It varies continuously during speech and consequently the pitch of the voice never remains the same for any appreciable time. This is the essential difference between singing and speaking, for in singing the pitch of the voice is held steady for the length of one note, whether long or short and changes of pitch are made between notes. The range of fundamental frequencies used in speech depends upon the individual speaker, with men using the lowest range, children the highest and women an intermediate range. These differences are reflected in the average fundamental frequency for the three classes of speaker: 120 Hz for men, 225 Hz for women and about 265 Hz for children. The total range of fundamental frequencies encountered in speech extends from about 60 Hz to about 500 Hz. In an individual speaker the range ordinarily employed is not more than one octave and this is located in the lower part of his total voice range.

One mode of vocal fold vibration must be treated as a special case in considering fundamental frequency; this is the type of production known as 'creaky voice' by British and as 'vocal fry' by American investigators. It is heard at the end of utterances where fundamental frequency falls to a low level and is characterized by the interspersion of larynx cycles of abnormally long duration; sometimes such cycles alternate with cycles of shorter period, so that there is a short cycle followed by a long cycle, followed by a short cycle and so on. If the period of these long cycles is converted to frequency, they represent fundamental frequencies in the range from 20 to 60 Hz. The phenomenon is common but by no means universal among speakers and these frequencies have not been taken into account in the estimates of fundamental frequency given above.

The most important function of variation in fundamental frequency is as a carrier of intonation. Both the grammatical intonation patterns which form a part of every language system and the emotional variations imposed by individual speakers are conveyed very largely by this means. Like all linguistic elements, intonation patterns have to be recognized in spite of all the differences introduced by individual speakers and they therefore depend on relations of fundamental frequency and not on the use of any standard pitch scale. They are tunes which can be sung in any key and indeed with any scale and we each of us choose those that suit our particular make-up. The factor which has the greatest weight, therefore, is the *direction* in which fundamental frequency changes with time, whether the pitch slides upwards or downwards and how rapidly it does so; after that the extent of the slide is important, but only in a rather gross way and in contrast with other patterns employed by the same speaker.

The circuits through which the brain controls speech activity enable us to adjust continuously the mass, length and tension of the vocal folds so as to produce the variations in larynx frequency corresponding to the intonation pattern we wish to convey.

Voice switching. A second linguistic function of larynx activity is connected with phonemic differences and contrasts. In running speech the vocal folds are vibrating for approximately 70 per cent of the time but owing to the occurrence of both voiced and voiceless consonants it is necessary for the vibratory activity to be switched on and off many times in the course of an utterance. The precise moment at which this switching takes place is very closely controlled by the speaker when he makes a distinction between pairs of voiced and voiceless sounds such as /p,b/, /t,d/, /k,g/, /s,z/ and so on.

Voice quality. The larynx waveform depicted in Fig. 28 is but one example of the kind of pulse wave that may be generated by vibration of the vocal folds. Since it has a particular arrangement of harmonics, that is a particular spectrum, it must constitute a particular sound quality. We can never actually hear the sound produced by a speaker's larynx because it does not become available to us until it has passed through his vocal tract and, as we shall see in the next chapter, been drastically modified by this transmission. It is, however, clear in principle that a change in larynx waveform must entail a change in quality. Individual speakers differ from each other in the formation and use of both the larynx mechanism and the vocal tract, but it has been established that differences in vocal fold vibration play a major role in enabling listeners to identify individual voices.

We have seen that within the speech of one individual there will be changes in the larynx wave with variation of fundamental frequency and of amplitude, particularly with regard to the ratio of the open to the closed phase of the cycle. The harmonic content of the wave will also vary according to the specific balance of mass, length and tension that is set up to produce a given frequency. The laryngeal muscles through which we adjust these factors are the medium by which we introduce into our speech the colouring expressive of our various moods and emotions, affection, bitterness, pleasure, disgust and so on. Each causes us to establish a different balance of forces in the larynx and hence to generate a different pulse wave, with different harmonic content and different sound quality. Similar differences, so extended in time as to constitute habitual modes of larynx action, characterize the voice and speech of individual speakers. When we refer to a speaker as a 'relaxed' or a 'tense' speaker, we are noting at least in part a difference in the extent to which physical tension is applied in the vibration of the vocal folds.

Summary of the larynx sound source

Vibration of the vocal folds, powered by air coming from the lungs during exhalation, is the sound source for voiced speech. It sets up a pulse wave in which the pulses are roughly triangular and of which the amplitude, fundamental frequency and waveform can be modified by the action of the laryngeal muscles. Mass, length and tension of the vocal folds are the physical factors which affect these variables; a speaker controls the balance between them in order to achieve the required effect at any moment. Fundamental frequencies in speech range from about 60 to 500 Hz but an individual speaker will not normally use more than about an octave. Men use the lowest fundamentals, women an intermediate range and children the highest. The switching on and off of vocal fold vibration is employed in the differentiating of voiced and voiceless sounds. The principal linguistic function of variation in fundamental frequency is the conveying of intonation patterns.

A triangular pulse wave has a spectrum in which all successive harmonics are present, with a progressive falling off of amplitude as frequency increases. Changes in fundamental frequency alter the spacing of harmonics in the spectrum but the general form of the amplitude spectrum remains approximately the same.

Apart from its role in conveying intonation and the voiced–voiceless distinction, the sound generated in the larynx does not transmit linguistic information. It acts as the carrier wave for this information which is imposed upon it by modifications introduced by the vocal tract; these modifications of the larynx wave are the subject of the following chapter.

7

The vocal tract

At the beginning of the previous chapter we saw that from the acoustic point of view the complete speech mechanism can be seen as a sound source coupled to a resonant system. The system is the air-way which leads from the larynx outwards through the pharynx and the mouth to the outer air, together with the path through the naso-pharynx and out through the nostrils when this branch is opened by the lowering of the soft palate. This is the system which is driven into forced vibrations by the pulse wave generated in the larynx. The sound waves radiated at the lips and the nostrils are the result of modifications imposed on the larynx wave by this resonating system. The first question therefore is: what are the properties of the vocal tract which determine these changes?

Forced vibrations, as we saw in Chapter 5, are the result of reflections and standing waves in the system, and these in turn are dependent on the natural frequencies and the damping of the system. It is these characteristics of the vocal tract that we need to examine.

Acoustic properties of the vocal tract

The example of the musical wind instruments showed that the dimensions of the air column involved were all-important in determining the frequencies at which resonance would occur. This must be so since the relation between the wavelength of sounds and these dimensions is the key to the phenomenon of resonance. The principle applies equally in the case of the vocal tract but the situation in speech is very much complicated by the fact that no two vocal tracts are the same size and shape and that short-term changes in the tract are brought about by articulatory movements. Communication by speech hinges on the fact that we learn to disregard the effects of the first and to pay close attention to the effects of the second type of variation.

In order to approach the problem of the acoustic performance of the vocal tract, we will begin with a drastic simplification of the conditions. The distance from the vocal cords to the lips in a male vocal tract is of the order of 17 cm. The area of any section across the tract varies greatly as we pass from the pharynx over the back of the tongue, under the hard palate and between the teeth but a representative area can be taken as 5 cm². Imagine the tract straightened out and formed into a cylinder of length 17 cm and cross-sectional area of 5 cm²; since the section is circular, the diameter will be 2.5 cm. This cylindrical tube has the vocal cords at one end and may be regarded as being closed here, but it is open at the other end, that is at the lips. For such a tube, the first resonance will be the frequency of which the tube length is equal to the quarter-wavelength, that is a sound whose wavelength is 68 cm. The velocity of sound in air is 340 m/s, so that this frequency is 500 Hz. This means that if we try to drive the air in the tube with a range of different frequencies, beginning with some low frequency, the tube will absorb a large proportion of the energy fed to it until our driving force gets into the region of 500 Hz and here we shall get a peak in the amplitude of the forced vibrations. How sharp this peak will be depends, as we know, on the damping of the system and this we will consider later on.

The resonance at 500 Hz is not likely to be the only one, and if we extend the range of the driving force we shall find, for a tube open at one end and closed at the other, a second resonance at a frequency of which 17 cm is three-quarters of the wavelength and a third of which 17 cm is one-and-a-quarter times the wavelength. Since frequency is inversely proportional to wavelength, we can find these frequencies very simply by multiplying the first, 500 Hz, by 3 and then by 5, giving 1500 and 2500 Hz. The amplitude of forced vibrations falls off as frequency rises and we should probably not discover any appreciable resonance above this. The principal resonances due to reflections along the length of the tube, therefore, would be at 500, 1500 and 2500 Hz. The diameter of the tube, 2.5 cm, could only produce reflection of frequencies whose wavelength was comparable with this distance. Since these would be very high frequencies, we should not expect this dimension to influence the resonance characteristics of the tube.

In the previous discussion of vibrating air columns we paid no attention to the question of damping. This factor concerns the absorption of sound energy and clearly absorption is the opposite of reflection. The air will exhibit the same damping wherever we find it (apart from small fluctuations brought about by changes in temperature and humidity) but

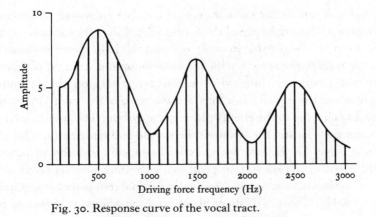

Fig. 30. Response curve of the vocal tract.

the material of the tube which encloses the air will have a great effect on the damping of the whole system. If the walls of the tube absorb a great deal of sound energy, the damping will be high and if they are efficient reflectors, there will be little damping. If therefore our cylindrical tube were made of glass or hard steel, the damping would be low, the system would be very selective or sharply tuned and the resonance peaks would be sharp. The material of the human vocal tract is of course rather the reverse of this; it is made of muscles and surface tissues, all of which are relatively absorbent and consequently the system will exhibit a high degree of damping. As we saw in Fig. 24, high damping results in a relatively flat resonance curve and the resonances of the vocal tract will be more of the form indicated in that figure than like the sharply tuned filter responses shown in Fig. 25. Because there is high damping, more energy will be absorbed generally and the overall amplitude levels will be reduced, but relatively there will be greater amplitude of forced vibration for the frequencies that intervene between the successive points of resonance. Consequently the three resonance curves will tend to join up with each other in the manner shown in Fig. 30. Each of the peaks indicates a resonance but the composite curve is most often referred to as a *frequency response curve* or *frequency characteristic* because it tells us how the particular system will treat a whole range of frequencies with which it may be driven. We must remember that the curve is obtained by joining up the highest points of lines giving the amplitude of spectrum components of the sound, in the way illustrated in the figure.

What the frequency response curve tells us is that when we drive the system with exactly the same amount of energy successively at different frequencies, the amplitude of the forced vibrations varies in accordance with the curve. Notice that in order to obtain this information we must be careful to drive the system with the same amount of energy, no matter what the frequency, otherwise we could not rely on the measured amplitude of the forced vibrations because some of the variations would be due to changes in the energy put into the system. The response curve specifies the acoustic behaviour of the system and remains valid for any driving force. In the case we are considering, the cylindrical tube of length 17 cm and cross-section 5 cm^2, with damping which approximates that of the human vocal tract, has three principal resonances at 500, 1500 and 2500 Hz. These will shape the forced vibrations or *output* of the system no matter what we drive it with. If the driving force is the larynx pulse wave, with the spectrum shown in Fig. 29, then the frequencies are all of different amplitude and the output will be the result of superimposing, as it were, the frequency response of the tract upon the spectrum of the glottal wave. In that case the output will have approximately the spectrum shown in Fig. 31(*a*).

The fundamental frequency of the larynx vibration in this example is 120 Hz and since all other frequencies in the complex tone must be multiples of this, there will not be a component at 500 Hz, which is the frequency of the first resonance of the tube. There is, however, a harmonic at 480 Hz which will show the greatest amplitude in the low part of the spectrum because of its proximity to the true resonance of 500 Hz. In the region of the second resonance of 1500 Hz, there is a component at 1440 and also at 1560 Hz. These are equidistant from the resonance but in the larynx spectrum 1560 Hz has lower amplitude than 1440 Hz and hence the latter will provide the second peak in the spectrum of the output. Near the third resonance there is a harmonic at 2520 Hz but there is also one of slightly greater amplitude at 2400 Hz; in the output spectrum we find two components of equal amplitude at this point, showing the presence of a true resonance between the two.

Let us now examine what happens when the fundamental frequency changes. Suppose that it rises to a value of 150 Hz. The components will now be the harmonic series 150, 300, 450, 600 Hz and so on. The lines in the spectrum will be more widely spaced and the peaks will appear at the places shown in Fig. 31(*b*), the first at 450 Hz, the second at 1500 Hz, since this is exactly the tenth harmonic of the fundamental, and the third at 2550 Hz. If the fundamental has a higher frequency still, let us say

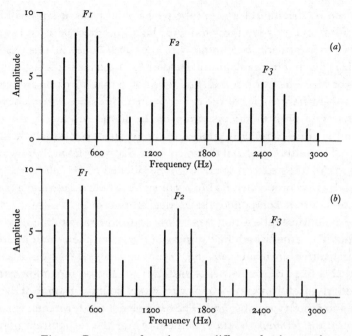

Fig. 31. Response of vocal tract to different fundamentals.

250 Hz, the spectral lines will be much wider apart still, but simple multiplication shows us that the resonances will fall exactly at 500, 1500 and 2500 Hz because there are harmonics of 250 Hz at each of these frequencies; they are the second, the sixth and the tenth harmonics.

In speech the fundamental frequency is changing all the time but the components of the larynx tone are always harmonics of the fundamental and the effect of the resonances of the tube or vocal tract is to produce a peak in the spectrum of the output at the harmonics which are the closest to the true resonance. This ensures that the spectrum of the resulting sound always has the same general outline or *envelope* although the fundamental frequency is continually changing. This fact is vitally important for speech because it means that a certain sameness of *quality* is heard in a range of sounds with different fundamentals. If this were not the case, speech sounds could not fulfil the linguistic function that they in fact have. The term used for a resonance of the system in this context is a *formant*. This is originally a German word used first by the physicist Hermann in the second half of the nineteenth century. The sound produced by driving the 17 cm tube we have been discussing will have three formants, at 500, 1500 and 2500 Hz. The practice is to assign a number to a formant, beginning with the lowest one; in this example 500 Hz is the first formant, abbreviated as F_1, 1500 Hz is the second, F_2, and 2500 Hz is the third, F_3. It should be noted that formants are strictly the resonant frequencies of the driven system but since a formant must give rise to a peak in the spectrum of the sound produced, the term formant is quite commonly applied to the frequency at which this peak occurs. Thus although F_1 of the 17 cm tube is at 500 Hz, in the spectrum of Fig. 31(*a*), the peak at 480 Hz might be labelled F_1; similarly the peak at 1440 Hz may be labelled F_2 but F_3 must lie between 2400 and 2520 Hz because these two components have equal amplitude.

The cylindrical tube is not a very close approximation to the real vocal tract but if it actually had the damping of the latter, then the sound with the first three formants at 500, 1500 and 2500 Hz would sound remarkably like a central vowel of the [əː] type. The notion of formants is particularly useful in connection with vowel sounds, though it can be applied to other types of sound. The arrangement of formants, what we may term the *formant structure*, is the basis for the recognition of most vowel differences. The peculiar property of the vocal tract is that its acoustic performance can be changed so as to bring about readily perceptible differences in formant structure. These changes are of course the result of differences in articulation which affect the shape and hence the dimensions of the vocal tract. The most important modifications are due to alterations in the configuration of the tongue. In the vocal tract itself the cylinder which has been used as an analogy is bent more or less into a right angle with a roughly vertical section in the pharynx and the back of the mouth and a roughly horizontal section in the front of the mouth. The body of the tongue can be moved backwards and forwards in such a way as to alter the relative length of the two sections and so change the resonances. The tongue also moves up and down and wherever it is highest in the mouth it forms a short tube which couples together the two sections of the vocal tract. The length and the cross-section of this tube have an influence on the formant structure of the sound and a further modification is introduced by the shape and the extent of the lip opening. Vowel systems in languages exploit all these means of creating differences in formant structure.

It must be stressed that the formant pattern of a particular sound is the outcome of the acoustic character of the whole tract working as one

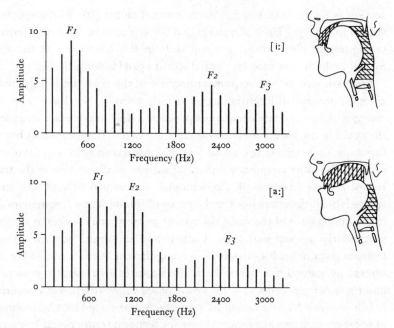

Fig. 32. Vocal tract shapes and spectra for [iː] and [aː].

resonant system. Hence it is not justifiable to assign any one formant to a particular part of the vocal tract. The frequencies of F_1 and F_2, for example, are interdependent since in general the lengthening of one section of the tract implies the shortening of the other. It is true, however, that the vertical section is longer than the horizontal and is therefore responsible for the wavelength of the lowest formant, F_1, while the shorter section tends to determine F_2. The interdependence is well illustrated by the contrast between the two vowels [iː] and [aː]. Fig. 32 shows the shape of the vocal tract and also typical spectra for these two sounds. For [iː] the front of the tongue is high in the mouth so that the rear section of the tract is very long, while the part in front of the tongue constriction is very short. This results in an F_1 of comparatively low frequency together with an F_2 of high frequency. The spectra are shown for a fundamental frequency of 120 Hz, with F_1 at a frequency of 360 Hz and F_2 at 2280 Hz. A change to the articulation for the vowel [aː] entails a completely different configuration of the vocal tract. The narrowing of the air column is now towards the back of the mouth, so that the vertical section is shorter, thus raising the frequency of F_1, and the horizontal section is longer, making F_2 much lower than for [iː]; in the spectrum shown in Fig. 32, F_I is at 720 Hz and F_2 at 1200 Hz. The difference in configuration also produces some shift in the frequency of the third formant which is at 3000 Hz for [iː] and at 2520 Hz for [aː].

Formant structure is important because of the role that it plays in the recognition and differentiation of speech sounds. We have seen that changes of fundamental frequency produce a shift in the exact location of the peaks in the spectrum because these are tied to the harmonics but the formants, that is the true resonances of the vocal tract, will lead to spectral peaks in the same frequency region for a given configuration of the tract, regardless of changes of fundamental frequency. There are quite appreciable differences both in the range of fundamental frequencies and in the dimensions of the vocal tract as we go from one speaker to another, particularly as between men, women and children, but the general formant pattern enables listeners to recognize the 'same' vowel when it is uttered by many different speakers. The vowel of *heed* will always have F_I and F_2 widely spaced and in the vowel of *hard* they will be close together.

It is possible by measuring enough spectra produced by a large sample of speakers to arrive at average values for formant frequencies. For vowel sounds generally, and this is true for the English system, a significant part of the information listeners use in distinguishing the sounds is carried by the disposition of F_I and F_2; Table 3 gives average values for F_I and F_2 for the pure vowels of English based on data obtained from a sample of English speakers. From these figures it is possible to see something of the systematic relationship between formant frequency and articulatory configuration. The first four vowel sounds form a progression from a close front to an open front articulation. We saw from Fig. 32 that the first of these causes a wide spacing between F_I and F_2. As the articulation is made more open, the air passage over the hump of the tongue becomes wider and the constriction also moves towards the back of the mouth cavity. These two effects together produce a gradual change towards the equalization of the vertical and the horizontal sections of the tract with a consequent shift of the frequencies of F_I and F_2 towards each other. When the point of articulation moves from front to back, as in going from the vowel of *had* to that of *hard*, there is a lowering of both formant frequencies. This apparently anomalous effect is explained by the fact that the tongue changes not only its position but also its shape; it can be bunched up so that the spaces both behind and in front of it become larger. The progression from open to close back vowel articulation produces a gradual reduction in the frequency of F_I; the sequence for F_2 is less regular as a result of the lip rounding which accompanies back vowels. The additional tube formed by the rounded lips lengthens the horizontal portion of the tract and lowers the second formant in comparison with an equivalent articulation with spread lips. This is particularly clear in the case of the vowel [oː] for which many English speakers use over-rounding of the lips; the mean frequency of F_2 is lower than for the neighbouring vowels. The two central vowels in the table, those of *hub* and *herb*, have formants which are intermediate between those of the front and the back vowels.

TABLE 3. *Mean frequencies of first and second formants of English vowels*

		F_I (Hz)	F_2 Hz)
iː	*heed*	300	2300
i	*hid*	360	2100
e	*head*	570	1970
a	*had*	750	1750
aː	*hard*	680	1100
o	*hod*	600	900
oː	*hoard*	450	740
u	*hood*	380	950
uː	*who*	300	940
ʌ	*hub*	720	1240
əː	*herb*	580	1380

(After J. C. Wells, 'A study of formants of the pure vowels of British English', unpublished M.A. Thesis, University of London, 1962.)

The articulation of diphthongs involves a tongue movement from the disposition for one vowel towards that for another and these sounds therefore give rise to a more or less rapid switching from one set of formants to another. The sound in the word *how*, for example, will begin with the formant frequencies for [aː] and these will then change smoothly in the direction of the formants for [uː]; the sound in *here* will begin with the formants for [i] and change in the direction of those for [əː] and so on for the other diphthongs. Just as the tongue movement in a diphthong is

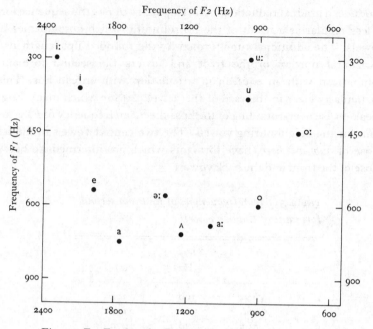

Fig. 33. *F1–F2* plots for English vowels.

not a complete change to a new vowel articulation but is rather in the nature of a glide in a given direction, so the modification of the formant frequencies may be of greater or less extent, depending upon the context and the speaker. It would therefore not be very meaningful to give mean formant frequencies for the elements in these sounds.

The relationship between articulation and formant structure has already been mentioned. This can be brought out rather strikingly by plotting a graph in which the frequencies of *F1* and *F2* for vowel sounds are represented on the two axes of the graph. The appearance of any graph is very much dependent upon the particular scales which are chosen for the related quantities; it may seem that those used in Fig. 33 are somewhat peculiar, but they are less so than they appear. The frequency scales for both *F1* and *F2* are logarithmic, that is to say that a multiplication of frequency is represented by the *addition* of a given distance on the scale. This serves to reflect more closely the impressions of relative pitch that a listener would gain; we saw earlier that the addition of equal pitch intervals requires the multiplication of the frequency of the stimulus by a given factor: an octave jump in pitch means a doubling of the frequency, for example. The fact that the frequency of F_2 increases. from right to left and that of F_1 from top to bottom of the graph does no more than determine the visual orientation of the pattern formed by the points that are plotted. Plotting the mean frequencies for the English vowels in this way in an F_1–F_2 space immediately shows up a resemblance in general outline between the acoustic structure of the sounds and their articulatory character as it is reflected in the conventional vowel quadrilateral. Close front vowels, as we have already noted, have a low F_1 and a high F_2; the distance between F_1 and F_2 decreases as we progress through the front vowels towards the open front articulation. The match between the vowel quadrilateral and the F_1–F_2 plot cannot be exact because the former takes account only of the point of greatest tongue constriction while the formant structure is influenced also by the position of the whole tongue in the mouth and by the lip shape. These factors affect the back vowels in particular and here we see the greatest differences between the two representations; the F_1–F_2 plot for [ɔː], for example, shows a low F_2 because of the lip-rounding.

It is therefore the acoustic characteristic of the whole vocal tract which modifies the wave generated at the larynx and hence shapes the sound which comes from the speaker's mouth. What makes the speech mechanism unique as a producer of sound is the fact that it is capable of an infinity of such modifications owing to the great flexibility of the articulators. We shall look at more of these possibilities in a later chapter when we come to examine in detail the acoustic characteristics of the various classes of sound in English. Before doing so, however, we must return to the subject of the generation of sound in speech, for we have so far considered only the vowel sounds, which normally depend upon larynx vibration as the sound source. There is a whole range of sounds, which include the voiceless consonants, which call for a quite different mode of operation.

8

Periodic and aperiodic sounds

All the sounds discussed so far have one feature in common: they consist of a fundamental frequency plus a series of harmonics. By definition, the frequencies of harmonics are always exact multiples of the fundamental frequency and every complex tone we have considered is a mixture of frequencies which satisfy this condition. One important implication of this concerns the wavelength and hence the waveform of the sound. If the fundamental frequency is 100 Hz, then the period of this vibration is 10 ms, that is to say it will cause a peak of compression every 10 ms and the peaks will be separated in space by the distance traversed in this time by sound waves in the given medium (in air, 3.4 m). The waveform of the vibration will be as it is shown in Fig. 3. The second harmonic, 200 Hz, will perform exactly two cycles in the same time and when the vibration at the fundamental frequency is passing through the position of rest to begin the second cycle, the second harmonic is also about to start on the positive half of its cycle. Similarly the third, the fourth, the fifth and indeed any other harmonic will complete an exact number of cycles in the time taken by one cycle of movement at the fundamental frequency. The result is that when all the different motions are combined to give the complex wave, exactly the same pattern of movement takes place within each cycle of the fundamental and the sound has a repeating waveform, as we saw illustrated in Figs. 11 and 12. Because of the regularly repeating character of the wave-motion, such a sound is said to be *periodic*. The musical sounds we have used as examples, including the pure tones, the sound generated by the larynx and the same sound modified by the vocal tract and issuing from the speaker's mouth as a vowel sound, all these are periodic sounds. Although periodic sounds may differ from each other in quality, as we have seen because of different arrangements of harmonics, the periodicity does produce a certain common character which is recognized by the ear and brain. Sounds which belong to the general class of periodic sounds are called *tones*; one feature of tones is that they have a definite pitch which is easily recognized.

Suppose that we encounter a sound in which not all the components are harmonics. We will take a hypothetical example in which the fundamental frequency is again 100 Hz and there are a number of harmonics of this frequency but there is also a component whose frequency is 227 Hz. The period of this vibration is approximately 4.4 ms so it will complete two cycles in 8.8 ms and when the fundamental embarks on its second cycle at time = 10 ms, it will already have done just over one-quarter of its third cycle. The addition of this wave-motion to the complex will give rise to a certain waveform for the first cycle of the fundamental. During the second cycle the situation will be different because the 227 Hz component will complete four cycles by time = 17.6 ms and will therefore have performed over half of its fifth cycle by time = 20.0 ms when the fundamental completes its second cycle. This will make the waveform of the second complex cycle different from the first. In each succeeding cycle the 227 Hz component will bear a different time (or phase) relation to the fundamental and all its harmonics and consequently the waveform of each cycle will be different and the exact periodicity will be destroyed. Such a component in a complex sound is called an *inharmonic* component and the complex is strictly speaking *aperiodic*. How far an inharmonic component changes the quality of an otherwise harmonic sound depends upon its amplitude; if the amplitude is low, the ear and brain will take little notice of its presence and hear the sound still as a tone.

The term aperiodic is more generally applied to sounds which are without any harmonic basis, that is in which the component frequencies are not related to each other as are the terms in the harmonic series. If one were to take a succession of truly random numbers and to generate frequencies corresponding to these values, the resulting complex sound would be aperiodic. There would be no simple numerical relationship between the frequencies and the waveform of the sound would show no discernible repeating pattern. It might appear that the occurrence of such a sound in the real world would be rare but nature in fact provides more examples than one might expect. Aperiodic sounds are those which the ear and brain class as *noises*; the sound of escaping steam and the sound of something being fried in a pan are good examples of natural noises. The essence of the contrast between a noise and a tone is the random nature of the air particle movement in the former and the regular, patterned

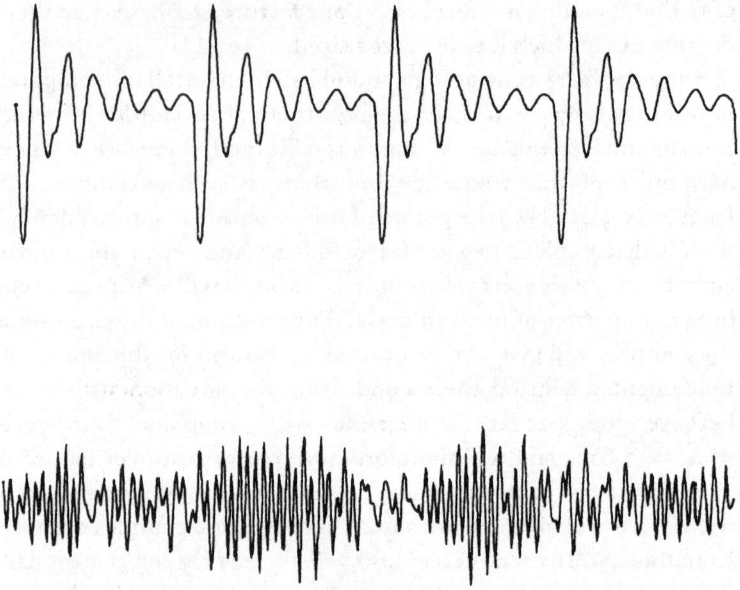

Fig. 34. Waveform of [aː] and of [s].

character of the movement in the latter. One method by which random movement may be set up is by forcing air to flow through a relatively narrow gap; this gives rise to *turbulence*, the phenomenon involved in most of the noises which occur in speech. In order to pronounce an [s] sound, we make a narrow constriction between the tongue and the teeth ridge and compel air to flow rapidly into this gap; the resulting turbulence produces a hissing sound with a waveform which is non-repeating, aperiodic. Fig. 34 shows a typical waveform for [s] compared with that for the vowel [aː]. Only a short stretch of each sound is shown but the time segments are equal in length and while the repeating pattern is obvious in the case of the vowel sound, it is not possible to see any signs of a pattern in the noise waveform.

For all the periodic sounds that occur in the course of speech the sound source is the larynx; the pulse wave set up by the opening and closing of the vocal folds provides the basic periodicity. The larynx can, however, act as a noise generator, as it does in whispered speech. If the glottis is narrowed so that the airway between the edges of the vocal cords is constricted without being completely obstructed, then turbulence will be set up at this point when the airflow from the lungs reaches a certain velocity. The constriction may be effected by leaving a space between the vocal processes of the arytenoid cartilages while bringing the remaining length of the cords into contact; this is the mechanism used in a strong or 'stage' whisper; or there may be a narrow opening between the cords along their whole length, including the vocal processes, as is the case in a gentler, more confidential type of whisper.

In whispered speech, then, the source of periodic sound is replaced by a noise source located at the same place. Whispered speech, provided that it is audible, is perfectly intelligible and this means that the noise source is just as effective in exciting the resonances of the vocal tract as the periodic or voice source, for it is upon these changing resonances that the intelligibility of speech depends. A whispered vowel has formants in the same frequency regions as the corresponding voiced vowel and in fact the effect of the formants can be more easily heard when a vowel is whispered. The resonances are evoked in a similar way in voiced speech when the consonant sound [h] is produced; the initial sound in the words *heed*, *hard*, *hoard* and *hood* has a different quality in each case because the vocal-tract resonances are different; each is in fact a gently whispered version of the succeeding vowel.

Whisper is a rather special case of noise generation in speech but voiced speech itself requires the setting up of noise sources for all the voiceless consonant sounds and in order to discuss these we need to consider some of the general characteristics of noise. The contrast between tone and noise is one which our ear and brain recognizes very readily as a difference in sound quality, even though there may be some sounds which we feel to be on the borderline between the two classes. A sound which arises from the random movement of air particles without any hint of periodicity strikes us as being noise without any doubt or qualification. The two examples given, of escaping steam and of hot fat in a pan, not only show a waveform with no repeating pattern but, if the sound is acoustically analysed, it is found to be made up of a very wide range of frequencies, all of more or less equal amplitude. It is possible by the use of electronic circuits to generate a noise consisting of all frequencies from, say, 20 to 20 000 Hz, that is covering the audible range, in which all the components have equal amplitude; such a noise is referred to as a *white noise*, by analogy with white light, which contains light of all wavelengths. The turbulence set up by forcing air at high speed through a narrow constriction produces a sound with the general character of white noise, though it may not conform exactly with the theoretical specification.

There is a second class of sounds which the ear recognizes as noises. Tones are characterized by a regularly repeating waveform; if the ear is struck by a single disturbance which is short-lived and not repeated, this too will be heard as a noise. Such sounds as a pistol shot, a single handclap and a click in a telephone earpiece are all noises because they have this feature; the waveform in each case is a single excursion. In response to such a noise the eardrum is forced in and out just once; when a tone arrives, it is forced in and out repeatedly but the repetition must be at a certain minimum rate for the impression of tone to be created. When a tuning fork of frequency 100 Hz is sounding, the wave forces the eardrum in and out every hundredth of a second; the effect in the sensory nerves of the first push and pull of the wave does not die away before the arrival of the second, and so on, and therefore the sensation fuses into that of a continuous tone. This is analogous to the visual phenomenon which enables us to see a series of still pictures as a moving film; provided the pictures are presented to our eyes at a rate not less than about 16 frames a second, we see continuous movement in the images. If the rate falls much below this, we see the film flicker and at very low rates we see a succession of still pictures. In the case of the ear, the limit for the fusion of successive impulses into a continuous tone is in the region of 30 Hz. Pipe organs may produce their lowest note from a pipe which is 16 feet long, giving a frequency of 33 Hz which just fuses into a tone. A large organ with a 32 foot pipe can generate 16 Hz and this is definitely heard as a series of pulses rather than as a continuous tone.

The noises which occur in speech include both the single disturbance or *transient* type, in the plosive consonant sounds, and the longer-lasting type in the fricatives and affricates. All of these require the setting up of a noise source at some point along the vocal tract. Whereas the source of periodic sound in speech is always at the larynx, the noise source for consonants may be sited at many different places in the tract, the location corresponding to what is referred to phonetically as the point of articulation of the sound. Thus noise is generated for [p, b] at the lips, for [f, v] at the lower lip, for [θ, ð] at the upper teeth, for [t, d] at the teeth ridge and at almost the same place for [s, z], while [ʃ, ʒ] have the noise generator a little further back; for [k, g] noise is generated at the soft palate and for [h] alone in the larynx.

When a consonant sound is voiced, this means that the tone generator in the larynx is working at the same time as a noise generator at some other point in the vocal tract; there are in fact two sources of sound. For example the sound [z], when it is being voiced as it is in the intervocalic position in English, calls for the operation of the periodic sound generator in the larynx and the noise generator at the alveolar ridge. Such sounds are therefore a mixture of tone and noise; their waveform cannot be strictly a repeating pattern because of the noise component, but a degree of periodicity is evident and it is this element which enables us to hear differences of pitch in these sounds.

The vocal tract as noise filter

It is clear from the example of whispered speech that the resonances of the vocal tract must operate on noise as they do on the periodic sound from the larynx, and therefore any noise generated in the tract will be greatly modified by the time it issues from the speaker's mouth. The resonating system works as a whole, that is to say that the resonances it imposes on the signal are the effect of the disposition of the whole length of the tract. This remains true no matter at what point a noise generator may be located; the section of the vocal tract both behind and in front of the constriction play their part in determining how the noise will be modified by the system.

If the noise generated is basically of the white noise type, the most noticeable effect of the vocal tract will be a drastic reduction in the amplitude of noise energy over certain frequency bands. For this reason it is usual to speak of the *filtering* effect of the vocal tract where noise is concerned. We saw in an earlier chapter (p. 58) that the concept of the filter is derived from one aspect of resonance.

The location of a noise generator in the tract affects the dimensions of the sections of the tract, behind and in front of the constriction, and this determines the resonances and hence the filtering effects introduced by the tract. An alveolar point of articulation divides the tract into a very short front section and a long rear section while a velar articulation divides the tract into almost equal lengths. The filtering effects are physically very complex and depend not only on the lengths of the sections of the tract but also on the length and the cross-sectional area of the constriction and on the rate of airflow. All of these factors enter, for example, into the filtering differences between an [s] and a [ʃ] sound. In the former the noise is filtered so that only components from about 4000 Hz upwards have any considerable energy while in the latter there is energy over a wide band from about 1800 Hz upwards.

In the case of plosive consonant sounds, the release of air pressure results in a very short burst of noise and this again is shaped by the vocal tract filter. In [t, d] the noise burst we hear is largely influenced by the short front section of the tract and is in the high frequency region at about 4000 Hz, while in [k, g] the noise is at a mid-frequency, in the region of 1800–2000 Hz.

A later chapter will give an acoustic description of all the sounds of English, including the consonants which involve noise components. The latter all exemplify the principles which have been outlined in this chapter, that is they are either long-lasting noises, the result of turbulence, filtered by the vocal tract, or they are short bursts of noise resulting from exciting the resonances of the tract by the sudden release of air pressure built up behind a complete occlusion of the airway. Both classes include examples, the voiced fricatives, affricates and plosives, in which noise generation is accompanied by the generation of periodic sound in the larynx.

9
Acoustic analysis: the sound spectrograph

The basic concepts of acoustics introduced in the first part of this book provide what is necessary for the specification and description of sounds of all kinds, including those of speech. The simplest possible account of a sound which reaches our ears is given by registering the amplitude of movement of an air particle which stands in the path of the sound wave; the movement changes continuously with time, both in direction and in distance travelled, and a graph of these variations is of course the waveform of the sound. Only the dimensions of time and displacement are involved in such a graph but if we note the time interval between reversals in the direction of movement or between the repetitions of a complex pattern of movement, then we introduce the dimension of frequency. We saw in Chapter 2 that any complex wave can be formed by the addition of sine waves of the appropriate frequency and amplitude and, where necessary, phase. The most practically useful account of any type of sound wave is that which specifies the frequency and amplitude of the component sine waves and the process which arrives at this information is that of *acoustic analysis* or *frequency analysis*. This chapter will be mainly concerned with the description of the most commonly used instrumental method of performing an acoustic analysis. Before embarking on this, however, we need one extension to the basic ideas which have been introduced so far.

Sound intensity
We have seen that no vibratory movement and therefore no sound is possible without a supply of force or energy; further we know that the total amount of force supplied to a system decides how much energy there is available to be used up or *dissipated* in vibratory movement of the system itself or in the movement of air particles which constitutes the sound waves. So far we have alluded to the 'strength' of a

sound only in terms of *amplitude* and we have seen that *loudness* depends on amplitude. We now have to modify this by saying that loudness is more nearly related to the energy in the sound. It is readily understandable that vibrations of greater amplitude require more energy than those of less amplitude and we know that the sound provided by the former will be the louder. But it is also intuitively understandable that if we have two sound waves of equal amplitude with one of them a higher frequency than the other, then more energy will be needed for the higher frequency, since the to-and-fro motion is taking place more often; if there were an octave difference in pitch, they would be taking place twice as often. In this second case, the higher frequency sound would also be the louder, despite the fact that the sounds are equal in amplitude. The loudness therefore depends rather on the energy in the sound and this is proportional to both the amplitude and the frequency. We need in fact a quantity which will take account of both of these, and the term for this is *sound intensity*. The relation between intensity on the one hand and frequency and amplitude on the other is not absolutely simple because intensity is proportional to the square of the frequency and to the square of the amplitude. This means that if we have a sound of frequency 100 Hz and we double the amplitude, the intensity will be four times as great; if we increase the amplitude threefold, the intensity will increase nine times and so on. Again, if we have sounds of differing frequencies but with the same amplitude, the intensities will vary with the square of the frequency and a 200 Hz tone will have four times the intensity of a 100 Hz tone, a 400 Hz tone will have sixteen times the intensity of the 100 Hz tone and so on.

The concept of sound intensity is particularly useful in view of the fact that all the sounds we have to deal with, certainly in speech, are complex sounds so that their intensity does not bear any simple relation to the amplitude or frequency of any of the components. There are electronic instruments for measuring sound intensity directly but, in the practical case, what is most often of interest is to be able to compare the intensities of two different sounds, for example the noise from a supersonic aircraft with that from a subsonic aircraft. It is for such purposes that the unit called the *decibel* has been defined, and since it has certain peculiarities it is necessary to give a detailed account of its nature and use.

The decibel

Two basic facts about the decibel have to be borne in mind:

the first is that it expresses a relation between two quantities, that is a ratio; the second is that it is a logarithmic unit, that is to say that the ratio is not expressed simply by saying that one quantity is four times the other, but by giving the logarithm of the ratio. We will see a little later the reason for this and how it works out in practice.

Since the purpose of measurement in decibels is to enable us to compare intensities, it is of course reasonable to give the answer in the form of a ratio. Basically we need to measure the intensity of the first sound, and we can call this quantity I_1, then to measure the intensity of the second sound, I_2, and work out the ratio of the two quantities. Intensities can be measured in some convenient units, for example watts, which are the units used to measure electrical power, as in the case of a 100 watt light bulb. The energy in sound waves is, however, extremely small compared with other forms of energy that we are familiar with; it has been estimated that it would require more than three million voices all talking at once to produce power equivalent to that which lights a 100 watt lamp. The ear and its associated system of nerve fibres form a receiver designed to deal with the very low levels of energy found in sound waves. The faintest sound which the average ear can detect can be generated with no more than 10^{-16} watts (0.000 000 000 000 000 1 watts). If a very high level of sound energy is applied to the ear it produces a sensation which is no longer that of hearing but of pain. This level is reached with approximately 10^{-4} watts (0.0001 watts). Compared with many non-acoustic forms of energy this is still a very low value, but the important point is that the whole range of sound intensity, from the faintest detectable sound to that which causes physiological pain, is represented by a ratio of one million, million to one.

The prevalence in acoustic work of such large numbers is a basic reason for the second feature of the decibel, its logarithmic nature. Any number can be expressed as a power of 10; thus 100 is 10^2, 1000 is 10^3, 1 000 000 is 10^6 and so on. In each case the index gives the logarithm to the base 10 of the number, so that log 100 = 2.0, log 1000 = 3.0, log 1 000 000 = 6.0, etc. Numbers which are not exact powers of 10 have logarithms which can be found by consulting tables of logarithms; thus the number 2 expressed as a power of 10 is $10^{0.3}$ and log 2 = 0.3; similarly, log 4 = 0.6, log 8 = 0.9, log 20 = 1.3. When this method was first used in expressing the ratio of sound intensities, the unit adopted was simply the logarithm of the intensity ratio 10:1, to which the name *bel* was given to commemorate the work of Alexander Graham Bell, the inventor of the telephone. It was found in practice that this unit was too large and it was replaced by the *decibel*, equal to one-tenth of a bel. In order to compare two sound intensities we must of course first measure both to find the ratio, I_1/I_2, placing the larger value in the numerator. The difference between the two sounds is then equal to

$$10 \times \log \frac{I_1}{I_2} \text{ decibels (dB)}.$$

Using this formula, we can see that if we are dealing with two sounds of which the intensity of one is 100 times greater than the other, then $I_1/I_2 = 100$, log 100 = 2.0 and 10 × 2.0 = 20 dB. When one intensity is twice the other, the log of the ratio is 0.3 and the difference is 3 dB. We saw that the difference in intensity between a sound which causes pain and the faintest audible sound was such that the ratio was one million million to one, that is 10^{12}; the log of the ratio is therefore 12 and the decibel difference is 120 dB.

There is a further reason for employing a decibel scale when dealing with sounds and that is that logarithmic units are more nearly in keeping with the changes in loudness sensation which result from increases in intensity; that is to say in order to add a constant amount of loudness we have to multiply the intensity by a constant factor, just as in the case of pitch we had to multiply the frequency in order to add a given pitch interval. Thus if we listen to two sounds, *A* and *B*, whose intensities differ by 20 dB, then the intensity of the louder sound, *B*, will be 100 times that of *A*; if we now want to produce a sound, *C*, which is louder than *B* by the same amount, we should need one which was 20 dB higher in intensity than *B*, in other words whose intensity was 100 times that of *B* and therefore 10 000 times that of *A*. When inferring from decibel differences to intensity ratios we have to be careful to keep in mind this relation between adding decibels and multiplying intensities. If a sound source is giving out a sound of a given intensity, for instance the high-intensity sound of a pneumatic drill, then by starting up a second drill we should raise the total intensity by only 3 dB since we have done no more than double the intensity. The same thing would hold good in the case of faint sounds; the intensity of a quiet whisper from one person would be increased by 3 dB if a second person joined in and whispered at the same time.

An increase in intensity of one decibel means an intensity difference of one-quarter and this is just about the smallest difference that the average ear can appreciate, so that this is another respect in which the decibel scale is linked to sensations of hearing as well as expressing the relations of physical stimuli.

The decibel as a unit of measurement has now become almost as familiar as the metre and the kilogram because of its use in the popular press as well as in technical literature. It may be difficult from the common usage to understand the insistence in the preceding paragraphs on the fact that decibels always express a ratio, for we frequently come across statements that the level of such-and-such a noise is x dB, with no reference to a second sound with which the noise is being compared. These statements do, however, invoke a concealed ratio because they imply that the noise intensity in question is being compared to a standard sound intensity, 10^{-16} watts which is approximately the threshold intensity for hearing. (In technical literature this reference level is often given as the equivalent sound pressure, which is 0.0002 dynes/cm^2.) Thus a noise which is said to be 90 dB has an intensity which is 90 dB higher than the level of 10^{-16} watts; the ratio of the intensities is one thousand million to one.

Our ears tell us plainly that the intensity of a sound falls off as we move away from the source. On flat ground in the open air or in any place where there are no reverberations, sound intensity decreases with the square of the distance; that is to say if we double the distance from the sound source, we shall receive one-quarter of the intensity, if we treble the distance, we shall receive one-ninth the intensity and so on. When the intensity level of a sound is given, therefore, it is important to specify the distance from the source, though this information is quite often not provided. Table 4 gives a list of some typical sound intensity levels in decibels above the common reference intensity of 10^{-16} watts.

Measurements such as those given in the table are made by using a sound-level meter, an electronic instrument in which sound waves are converted into electrical variations by means of a microphone and amplifier and the intensity is read upon a dial calibrated in decibels with reference to the required standard. Values given in this way must of course be the average of a number of readings and the conditions represent average or typical conditions. The intensity of conversational speech, 3 ft from the speaker, for instance, is shown as 60 dB. This is a representative or average value in two senses. Speakers vary a good deal in the volume at which they normally converse, so that any individual speaker is not very likely to give exactly this measurement, but in

TABLE 4. *Decibel scale of common sound intensities*

Intensity (dB)	Sound
130	4-engined jet aircraft, 120 ft
120	Threshold of pain; pneumatic hammer, 3 ft
110	Boilermakers' shop; 'rock' band
100	Car horn, 15 ft; symphony orchestra, *fortissimo*
90	Pneumatic drill, 4 ft; lorry, 15 ft
80	Noisy tube train; loud radio music
75	Telephone bell, 10 ft
70	Very busy London traffic, 70 ft
60	Conversation, 3 ft; car, 30 ft
50	Quiet office
40	Residential area, no traffic: subdued conversation
30	Quiet garden; whispered conversation
20	Ticking of watch (at ear); broadcast studio
10	Rustle of leaves
0	Threshold of audibility

addition, as we saw earlier, the amplitude and therefore the intensity of successive speech sounds varies considerably owing to the syllabic structure of the speech sequence. The figure of 60 dB is therefore an average for a number of speakers and also an average over some stretch of conversation, taking into account the syllabic variations in intensity. If speakers speak as loudly as they can, are in fact shouting, this average figure, again measured at a distance of 3 ft, rises by about 15 dB to 75 dB. In very quiet speech, which is still voiced and not whispered, the level drops to about 35–40 dB.

From this point onwards we shall generally refer to the intensity of speech sounds rather than to their amplitude and we shall use the decibel as the unit in comparing sound intensities.

The technique of frequency analysis

In Chapter 5 we saw that the composition of a complex tone expressed in terms of the fundamental and harmonic frequencies and the relative strength of the components is referred to as the spectrum of the sound and a number of examples were shown of a common method of representing the spectrum graphically (see for instance Fig. 26). Such a summary of the acoustic nature of speech sounds and of many other kinds of sound is so useful that some technique for arriving at and drawing a sound spectrum is indispensable, and this is provided by the sound spectrograph.

The requirements are that the instrument shall take in the sound waves, detect the various frequencies of which it is made, measure their relative intensities and translate the results into a visible form. In the spectrograph, as in all other sound registering devices, the first stage is that sound waves are picked up by a microphone, which converts the movement of air particles into electrical variations and these variations are suitably amplified. At this point the input to the system is still in the form of the complex wave. The essence of the sound spectrograph is the operation which analyses this wave into its component frequencies. This is effected by the use of electronic filters. We noted earlier that a filter is really a resonator looked at from one particular point of view; when we think of resonance we are more concerned with the frequencies which are favoured by the resonator, whereas in the filter attention is directed more to the frequencies which are rejected, but the operation is the same in both cases and electronic filters are in fact resonant circuits. A suitable arrangement of electronic components will form a circuit which will admit or *pass* frequencies within a certain band with very little loss of energy but will drastically reduce the energy of any frequencies on either side of this band. A filter of this kind is called a *bandpass* filter and its performance is specified by giving the frequency limits within which a signal will be passed with very little loss of energy. A filter might, for example, pass frequencies from 135 Hz to 180 Hz and reduce frequencies on either side of these values to a very low intensity. The band between these two frequencies is 45 Hz wide and this is termed the *bandwidth* of the filter. Filters can be arranged so that their pass bands are adjacent to each other; they are placed as it were side by side across the frequency range and each filter registers the amount of energy contained in the complex tone which falls within its own pass band. Each filter is followed by an electronic circuit which measures and then registers this level of energy. Let us imagine a device with such a range of filters, each with a bandwidth of 45 Hz. We send into the microphone the sound of a sustained vowel [aː] on a fundamental frequency of 100 Hz. The sound contains no energy below this frequency so that the first two filters, those covering the band 0–45 Hz and 49–90 Hz will detect no energy and register no output. The third filter, whose pass band is 90–135 Hz, will register the intensity of the fundamental. The next harmonic in the sound is at 200 Hz and the intensity of this component will be registered by the fifth filter, band 180–225 Hz; no energy will pass through the fourth filter, whose pass band falls between the fundamental and the second harmonic. Similarly throughout the frequency range, wherever a harmonic of the vowel sound falls within the pass band of a filter, that filter will have an output proportional to the intensity of the harmonic; all other filters will show zero output. From the earlier discussion we know that the highest levels of intensity will appear in the spectrum in the regions of the formant frequencies. Table 3 shows that for [aː], F_1 and F_2 will be close to 680 and 1100 Hz. Since our fundamental frequency is 100 Hz, the spectrum peak for F_1 is likely to appear at 700 Hz, that is in the pass band of filter number 16, and F_2 will be in fact at 1100 Hz, in filter number 25; F_3 will most probably be seen somewhere between filters 50 and 55.

The sound spectrograph which is in most common use for speech work uses a filter bandwidth of 45 Hz, in one of its settings.* Instead of employing a bank of filters, it has an arrangement for continually re-tuning a single filter so that it 'looks at' successive frequency bands, but this does not change the end result. The intensity relations of the various components in the sound are measured as decibel differences. The maximum difference the filters will register is 30 dB. Any harmonics whose intensity is more than 30 dB below the highest peak in the spectrum will register as having zero intensity. In using the spectrograph some care has to be taken not to set the various volume controls too high because this overloads the system and causes a distortion of the spectrum. Fig. 35 shows two spectra drawn by a sound spectrograph, one for a vowel [aː] and the other for a vowel [e], both sustained on a fundamental of 100 Hz. It will be seen that harmonics are registered by the same filters in both cases but that relative intensities are different because of the change of formant structure as between [aː] and [e].

Such visible patterns provide us with important information about the sound coming from a speaker's mouth at a particular moment. They present a frequency analysis of the sound, with the frequency scale measured off on the horizontal axis and the relative intensity of the components in decibels shown on the vertical axis. By measuring the

---

* This is the commercially produced instrument called the Sona-Graph, manufactured by the Kay Electric Company, USA. The spectrograms obtained from this machine are sometimes referred to as Sonagrams.

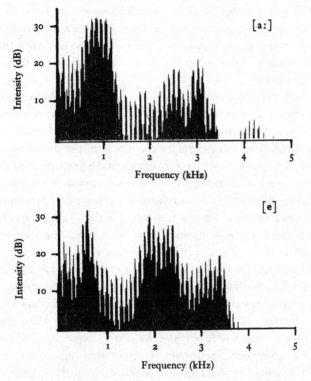

Fig. 35. Spectrograms of [aː] and [e], narrow band sections.

distance on the horizontal scale between successive harmonics we can arrive at the fundamental frequency of a periodic sound, since this must be equal to the frequency difference between one harmonic and the next in the series; differences in intensity between any frequency component and any other can be read off on the vertical scale.

The acoustic output from the speaker represents the periodic tone generated by the larynx modified by the resonance characteristics of the vocal tract; the formants give rise to peaks of intensity in the spectrum like those which are apparent in the patterns of Fig. 35. But we know that the resonances of the vocal tract are changing all the time in speech because of the continual movements of the tongue and the other articulators and consequently each display in the figure only depicts the situation at one instant during the production of a vowel sound. It corresponds, as it were, to a single still picture out of what should be a moving film. For this reason such a pattern is called, in spectrographic terms, a *section*. To gain an adequate idea of the acoustic variations that take place in the course of a speech sequence, we need to be able to follow the changes in spectrum as time passes. This we can do by using the spectrograph in another mode, that in which it produces a three-dimensional spectrogram.

We will begin with a very simple sequence, the syllable /ai/. At the start of this utterance the vocal tract is disposed as for a vowel of the [aː] type and will therefore have the formants and the spectrum for this sound. As time passes the articulation changes relatively slowly in the direction of that for a vowel of the [i] type, in which formants 1 and 2 are separated by a greater frequency interval than for [aː]. The spectrograph, working in three-dimensional mode, enables us to follow this change and produces the pattern shown in Fig. 36. Here the frequency scale is transferred to the vertical axis instead of the horizontal; the relation can be seen by imagining the patterns of Fig. 35 turned through 90° so that low frequencies are represented at the bottom and high frequencies at the top of the vertical scale. The horizontal axis is now used for the measurement of time, as in nearly all of the graphs in the earlier chapters, and is marked off in intervals of one-tenth of a second or 100 ms. What then has happened to the measurement of intensity? We can no longer read off the decibel differences between frequency components but intensity variations are still indicated by the degree of darkness of the trace made in the pattern. The background of the pattern is light grey and wherever this tone appears it denotes zero sound intensity; where the trace is dark, this denotes maximum intensity. The first feature we notice is a number of broad, dark bands running across the pattern, together with a series of more or less horizontal lines. Each of these lines represents the energy present in successive harmonics of the periodic sound. The filter bandwidth of the device is 45 Hz, as before, and it therefore detects each harmonic separately and registers that there is zero intensity between harmonics. The broad bars are themselves made up of high-intensity harmonics and they show the effect of the formants. Beginning at the low end of the frequency scale, the first bar denotes the presence of F_1, the second of F_2 and the third of F_3. During the first part of the syllable, F_1 and F_2 are close together on the frequency scale, as we expect in a vowel of the [aː] type. If we estimate the position on the frequency scale of the mid-point of these two bars, we find that F_1 is at approximately 770 Hz and F_2 at approximately 1100 Hz. The change of articulation to the second element of the diphthong takes place quite gradually and by the

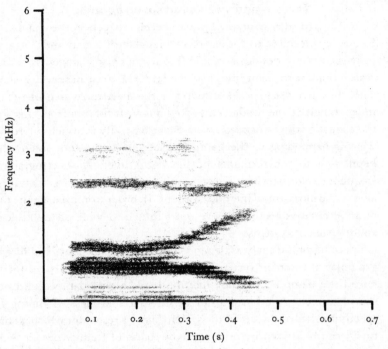

Fig. 36. Spectrogram of [ai], narrow band.

end of the syllable $F1$ and $F2$ are well separated in frequency, reaching values of approximately 440 Hz for $F1$ and approximately 1760 Hz for $F2$. The frequency of $F3$ remains relatively constant throughout the syllable at approximately 2400 Hz. The bar due to $F1$ is about four harmonics wide, that due to $F2$ is about three and the $F3$ bar is rather narrower and shows generally less intensity.

From the time scale we can read that the whole syllable occupies just a little more than 500 ms. The [aː] formant configuration takes up more than half of this time and the change to the second element goes on during most of the rest of the syllable, the [i] configuration occupying the last 100 ms.

This very simple example shows immediately the extreme usefulness of the spectrogram for the study of speech sounds for one can learn a great deal about a given utterance just by inspecting the pattern and one can also make quite reliable measurements of time and frequency. Measurements of intensity require additional techniques which will be described later.

Narrow- and wide-band spectrograms

In the course of any speech sequence the fundamental frequency produced by the larynx changes continuously and hence, as we have seen, the series of harmonic frequencies also changes. It is for this reason that the formants play such an important role in speech reception, since they give rise to peaks of energy in the spectrum which are relatively independent of the fundamental frequency. It follows from this that in the acoustic study of speech we are not basically so much interested in what is happening to the harmonics of the larynx tone as in what is happening to the formants of the vocal tract. A spectrographic or frequency analysis which registers individual harmonics is therefore not always the most useful method to adopt. In order to appreciate the nature of an alternative technique, we must return to some of the basic facts about resonant systems.

Spectrographic analysis depends upon the use of filters and filters are examples of resonant systems. Such systems may be sharply tuned and have little damping, or they may be more highly damped and not so sharply tuned. Another way of expressing sharpness of tuning is by specifying the bandwidth of the system, since a resonator which is sharply tuned can be driven by only a narrow band of frequencies; it will not respond to frequencies outside this narrow band. A resonator which is not sharply tuned, on the other hand, will respond to a much broader band of frequencies. A filter is a resonator and if it has a narrow bandwidth, it is sharply tuned. In this context a filter with a bandwidth of 45 Hz can be regarded as having a narrow bandwidth and as being therefore quite sharply tuned. Now the other characteristic of a sharply tuned system is that, once it is excited, it will go on 'ringing' for a comparatively long time, because it has little damping. Suppose that a filter of this nature is being used to register sounds and an input arrives which is within its band of frequencies. It will detect the arrival of this input but will then go on 'ringing' for some time because of the lack of damping. If during that time a second signal arrives, it will go undetected because the filter is still responding to the first or will simply add its effect to that of the first input and the two will not be distinguished. Contrast this with the behaviour of a system or filter which is highly damped. Any input which arrives will be detected and its effect will die away rapidly so that a second input arriving shortly afterwards will be detected as being separate from the first. The price that has to be paid, however, is that the second filter has a wide bandwidth and is therefore incapable of distinguishing two inputs which are close together in frequency. Thus we see that there is a relation between the capacity to detect and distinguish signals which are close together in time and those which are close together in frequency; the better the filter is at the first, the worse it will be at the second so that it becomes a matter of trading *time resolution* for *frequency resolution* and vice versa, according to the objectives of the measurements that are being made. The two are inversely proportional to each other, approximately. So far we have referred to the condition in which the spectrograph is using a narrow-band filter, with a bandwidth of 45 Hz; this means that its time resolution is of the order of 20 ms. If two events follow each other within a shorter interval than this, their effects will be added together and they will not be differentiated. The spectrograph which is in common use has an alternative arrangement in which the analysing filter has a bandwidth of 300 Hz. This means that the energy of all components within a band of 300 Hz will be added together, but on the other hand the time resolution will be close to 3 ms.

This interdependence of frequency and time analysis can perhaps be more easily grasped if it is expressed metaphorically in this way: the spectrograph takes in the whole sound input and its task is to tell us how much sound intensity there is at particular frequencies at different times. The filter system therefore has to slice up the sound into frequency slices and time slices; because of the nature of filters, this can be done by cutting thin frequency slices, but in that case we have to put up with rather coarse time slices (45 Hz frequency slices mean 20 ms time slices); or we can choose to have coarse frequency slices for the sake of having thin time slices (300 Hz frequency slices, but 3 ms time slices). It might seem that a time interval of 20 ms is already a very short period but in fact some of the acoustic events in speech happen very rapidly and will not be adequately registered unless the time resolution is rather better than this. To take just one example, the average larynx frequency for male speakers is 120 Hz. The time taken for one opening and closing of the vocal folds at this frequency is just over 8 ms and if we needed to look at any effects connected with successive openings and closings of the vocal folds, we should need time slices nearer to 3 ms than to 20 ms.

Some of the results of changing from a filter bandwidth of 45 Hz to one of 300 Hz can be seen by comparing Fig. 37 with Fig. 36. This is an analysis of exactly the same utterance as in Fig. 36 but made with the wide-band filter. The general features of the pattern are the same in the two cases, as indeed they must be if the analyses are to be of much use in

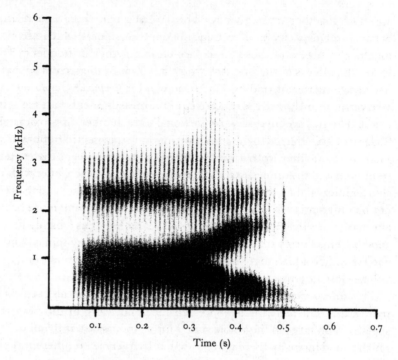

Fig. 37. Spectrogram of [ai], wide band.

the study of speech, but there are a number of important differences. The first is that whereas the narrow-band spectrogram (Fig. 36) is made up basically of horizontal lines, the wide-band spectrogram is composed of vertical striations. This is a visible indication of the differences in frequency and time resolution which we have just been discussing. The horizontal lines in the narrow-band spectrogram are the slices on the frequency scale; with a filter bandwidth of 45 Hz, the analyser 'sees' each successive harmonic and registers the drop in intensity between one harmonic and the next. This effect is absent in the wide-band spectrogram because with a filter band 300 Hz wide, the energy from several harmonics will fall within a single band. The fundamental frequency during this utterance is approximately 110 Hz so that the intensity of at least two harmonics will be added together in every band that is 'looked at' by the analyser. One consequence is that the formant bars appear somewhat broader and also darker in Fig. 37 than in Fig. 36. But the wide-band filter has better time resolution and can see events that succeed each other with intervals longer than 3 ms. With a fundamental frequency of 110 Hz, the opening and closing of the vocal folds occupies about 9 ms. Each time the folds open, there is a little burst of acoustic energy and when they close, this energy diminishes; the wide-band filter detects each successive event of this kind and hence vertical slices appear with respect to the time axis.

It has been found that for most purposes in the acoustic study of speech the wide-band analysis is more useful than the narrow-band. The next chapter will include a detailed discussion of the acoustic features of the sounds which make up the English sound system and we shall see in the course of this the importance of many short-lived events in speech.

Spectrographic analysis of noise

The utterance which has been analysed to give the spectrograms of Figs. 36 and 37 consists of voiced sound throughout, that is to say the sound is periodic from beginning to end. Hence the narrow-band pattern shows discrete harmonics and the wide-band pattern shows voice vibrations for the whole duration of the syllable. But not all speech sounds are periodic, as we have seen, and the spectrograph has also to deal with the noises which occur in speech. From the point of view of a filter, the distinction between periodic and non-periodic sound does not exist. Its only function in the spectrograph is to accept the sound input and measure the total amount of energy over a certain time. When we look at the spectrogram, we are able to tell from its appearance when the sound is periodic from the presence of harmonic lines or vertical striations in the two types of spectrogram. Noise arises from turbulence, that is the random movement of air particles, and the acoustic result is a continual switching from one frequency to another over a wide range of frequencies throughout the duration of the noise. At the same time, any noise generated in the vocal tract must excite the resonances of the tract, as we know from the example of whispered speech. These two features are illustrated by the spectrogram shown in Fig. 38 which is a wide-band analysis of the utterance [ai] whispered instead of voiced. The various filter bands receive energy haphazardly so that the regular striations of the previous pattern are replaced by random traces over the whole spectrogram, but there are still high levels of energy in the broad frequency bars which indicate the formants and the disposition of these changes with time just as in the voiced version of the utterance.

Noises which correspond with the occurrence of consonant phonemes in the phoneme string are naturally of shorter duration than a complete

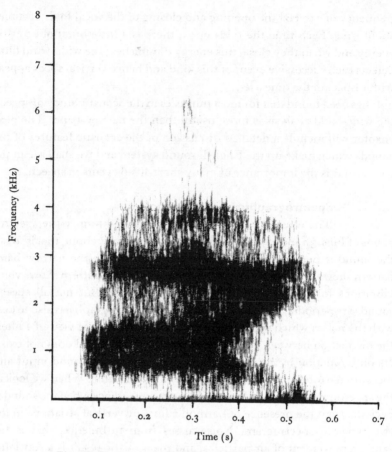

Fig. 38. Spectrogram of whispered [ai].

syllable and they often show clearly the filtering effect of the vocal tract. An utterance of the word *seashore* has been analysed to give the spectrogram of Fig. 39. The alternation of noise with periodic sound is obvious in the pattern and the difference between the filtering effects in the two noises is also evident. In the initial noise, there is practically no acoustic energy below approximately 4000 Hz whereas in the second, noise energy begins just below 2000 Hz. This accounts for the contrast between high-pitched and low-pitched noise in these two sounds.

When the explosive type of noise occurs in speech, particularly in the voiceless plosives [p, t, k], the closure of the vocal tract interposes a short silence, which must of course appear in the spectrogram as a blank patch, since there is zero sound energy to register. If the consonant is released,

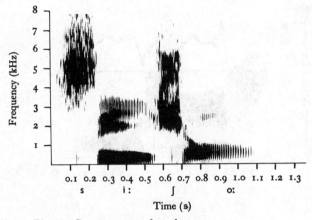

Fig. 39. Spectrogram of *seashore*.

there is a short burst of noise, that is a random patch of very narrow extent with reference to the time axis.

Where both the larynx tone generator and a noise generator are working at the same time, as in intervocalic voiced fricatives, the appearance of the spectrogram depends very much upon how strongly the sound is voiced and on the proportion of noise to tone in the particular utterance. Often the presence of voice striations can be seen only in the lowest frequency band and the rest of the spectrum has a typical noise appearance, but sometimes the noise patch itself has a somewhat striated appearance.

Measurement of intensity

Three-dimensional spectrograms, whether narrow-band or wide-band, allow us to gauge intensity differences in a qualitative way but do not permit measurements of relative intensity. By making *sections* of the type shown in Fig. 35 we can measure the relative intensity of the components of a sound and compare one harmonic with another or one formant with another. Such a section, however, represents a very short sample of the sound and it is difficult to establish how representative of the whole sound that sample is. Nonetheless sections made in the course of sounds which lasted for an appreciable time with little variation can provide useful information about the spectrum and can be used in comparing one sound with another. The spectra of friction noises can be arrived at just as well as those of periodic sounds.

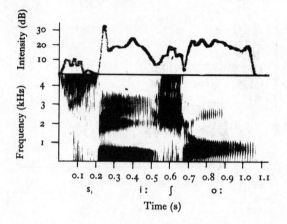

Fig. 40. Spectrogram of *seashore* with amplitude display.

The sound spectrograph usually provides a facility for making another type of intensity measurement, that of the variation in total sound intensity as an utterance progresses. The *amplitude display* draws a continuous curve which specifies the rise and fall in total intensity as the various sounds succeed each other. A curve obtained in this way is shown in Fig. 40 where the spectrogram of *seashore* is repeated with the intensity curve above it; the frequency analysis has been stopped at a lower frequency in order to allow room for the additional trace. The intensity differences can be read off the scale in decibels. As we expect, there is a main peak of intensity for each syllable and subsidiary peaks for the two fricatives. There is little difference in level between the two vowels, though the second, more open vowel is maintained at a slightly higher intensity than the first. Both fricatives are strong but the first is approximately 10 dB weaker than the second.

Information contained in the spectrogram

The sounds which make up the English sound system will be described in spectrographic terms in the next chapter, but it will be as well to summarize what has been said in this chapter by making a few general points about the interpretation of spectrograms. The most essential of these is the importance of realizing that it is not possible to cut up the patterns on the time axis and say 'This piece is the /b/, this piece is the /uː/, this is the /n/' and so on, because this implies that the first segment contains the acoustic information we use in recognizing the

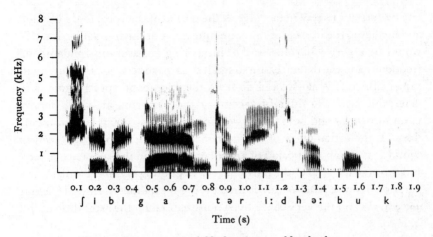

Fig. 41. Spectrogram of *She began to read her book.*

sound as /b/, etc.* The matter of the recognition and identification of speech sounds will be dealt with in a later chapter and there we shall see that the process is not as simple as a straightforward segmenting of the spectrographic patterns would imply. What we can derive from the spectrogram is reliable acoustic information about the events of speech and we can of course associate this with perception and recognition, but not in the direct way that we tend at first to believe is possible.

There are several basic distinctions to be made from inspection of the spectrogram; the first is that between sound and silence. A blank space in the pattern means that the sound has ceased; if it lasts more than about 150 ms this is due to a pause on the part of the speaker, but many shorter silences occur which are due to the articulation of plosive consonant sounds. A number of examples are to be seen in the spectrogram of the sentence *She began to read her book,* shown in Fig. 41. Some of the stops are very brief, that associated with /t/ is scarcely 20 ms, while that for /k/ is of the order of 115 ms.

The second distinction is that between periodic and aperiodic sound, in phonetic terms between voiced and voiceless sounds. The wide-band analysis provides a time constant short enough to allow it to detect successive openings and closings of the vocal folds and whenever vertical striations are apparent in the wide-band spectrogram, we are looking at a time during which there were larynx vibrations. The distance between

* In Fig. 41, the letters are placed so as to show approximately the sections of the spectrogram corresponding to the sounds in the sequence.

any two striations will in fact give us the period of the vocal fold vibration and by taking the inverse of this we could arrive at the frequency, but this would be a very laborious way of measuring variation in fundamental frequency and the distances are so small as to make accurate measurement rather difficult. What we can do from the wide-band spectrogram is to determine with considerable accuracy the moments at which larynx vibration starts and stops, and we can see when voicing is continuous through the articulation of a consonant. In Fig. 41, voicing is seen to continue through the period of articulation of [r] in the sequence *to read* and through the stop of the plosive at the beginning of *book*. Similarly the duration of noise patches can be measured, for example the initial friction noise in *she* and the very short-lived noise caused by the aspiration of the [t] in *to*.

The formant bars are well-defined throughout most of the sequence. In this connection, you will notice that at many places there is a rather rapid change in the frequency of a formant. This is often the case with F_2; the most obvious examples are where the syllable *she* is linked with the stop of the initial [b] of *began*, after the stop of [g] in the latter word, and in the linking of the word *to* with the word *read* by the articulation of [r]. Such rapid changes in formant frequency are referred to as formant transitions and we shall see later that they play an important role in the identification of speech sounds.

One thing which spectrographic analysis makes abundantly clear is that the acoustic aspect of speech is one of continuous change, as indeed it must be since it is the fruit of continuous movement on the part of the speech mechanism. Despite this fact, a great part of the basic knowledge which we have about speech acoustics has been gained through the inspection of spectrograms and through measurements made with their aid.

The sound spectrograph and scales of measurement

The sound spectrograph is a device which converts a sound input into a visible pattern and thus translates acoustic dimensions into distances which can be measured with a ruler. The conversion factors naturally depend upon the particular spectrograph which is being employed but as the Sona-Graph is in very wide use, it is worth while to deal briefly with the conditions in this instrument. If a section is made, the dimensions are frequency and intensity; if a three-dimensional spectrogram is made, whether narrow-band or wide-band, the dimensions of measurement are frequency and time, with intensity variations available only for qualitative judgment by inspection; if the amplitude display is used, the dimensions are overall intensity and time. It is usual to have some options concerning the relations between distance and the acoustic dimensions, in spectrographs generally and in the Sona-Graph. Here we will deal only with the standard arrangement which is most commonly used.

The frequency range of the analysis is 8000 Hz and the conversion factor is 2000 Hz = 1 inch on the recording paper, so that on the vertical axis the pattern extends over a distance of 4 inches. The frequency scale is linear, that is to say every increase of 2000 Hz is represented by a distance of 1 inch; this is not representative of our perception of pitch differences, for we saw in an earlier discussion that we perceive all octave differences as being equal. A scale which reflected this fact would use a standard distance for every octave, that is to say for every doubling of the frequency; it would be a logarithmic scale similar to the decibel scale.

In measuring frequency on the spectrogram we may reasonably expect to measure differences of one-fiftieth of an inch and since 1 inch = 2000 Hz, this means that the smallest frequency difference we can measure is 40 Hz. When dealing with periodic sounds, we know that successive harmonics are separated by an equal difference in frequency and this is useful information when estimating the frequency of a component, but it is only available in the case of narrow-band spectrograms, since separate harmonics are not registered in the wide-band pattern. In arriving at formant frequencies in wide-band spectrograms, it is a common practice to draw a line by eye through the middle of the formant bar and to make the frequency measurement by reference to this line.

The frequency scale in sections is the same as in the three-dimensional spectrograms and can be treated in the same way. The intensity scale is a logarithmic one since it measures relative intensities in decibels. The range of intensity which can be measured is nominally 33 dB and the conversion factor is 1 dB = 1 mm. In order to avoid distortion of the frequency components in the sound which is being analysed, it is necessary to set the volume control of the spectrograph so that the most intense component shall not reach the limiting value of 33 dB. The amplitude display uses the same intensity scale and in its use the same care has to be taken to avoid distortion.

The maximum time covered by a single spectrogram, in the case of the

Sona-Graph, is 2.4 seconds; the equivalent distance is 12 inches and therefore half an inch equals one-tenth of a second, or 100 ms. Again if we measure distances to one-fiftieth of an inch, we shall be measuring time differences to 4 ms.

The limits to our accuracy in measuring frequency, intensity and time from spectrograms that have been mentioned here are theoretical rather than practical. It is important not to form too optimistic an idea of the accuracy of spectrographic measurements; the stylus of the instrument traces a line of appreciable thickness and in addition we have to remember the time and frequency resolution of the analysing system, what is referred to as the integration time of the filters, about 20 ms for the 45 Hz and about 3 ms for the 300 Hz filter.

10

Acoustic features of English sounds

The sounds of speech are generated by the speech mechanism of a vast variety of different speakers, even if we confine our attention to the sounds of one language. All these speakers have a larynx and vocal tract of different dimensions, they have a different upbringing and different speech habits, a different emotional make-up and voice quality. Even one individual speaker talking at different times will produce sounds which are acoustically very different so that any utterance we may take for purposes of acoustic analysis can be only one sample out of millions of possible ones. Some impression of the extreme variability to be met with in utterances from any considerable number of different speakers can be gained from the plots in Fig. 42. These give the frequency of F_1 and F_2 for ten different vowels in utterances by 76 speakers of American English. Even here the variation is very much reduced by the fact that the analyses are of words spoken in isolation and not in running speech. It is clear that if we are going to be concerned with the acoustic analysis of speech sounds we must be prepared to encounter this degree of variability.

Because language systems work, however, despite acoustic variability, it is both useful and meaningful to make generalizations about the acoustic characteristics of the different classes of sound that make up a linguistic sound system. Many such general statements have been included in the discussion in preceding chapters; in this chapter we shall deal with English more systematically from this point of view and we shall direct attention more specifically to the kind of information to be obtained by the inspection and measurement of spectrograms.

English vowel sounds
All vowel sounds in normal speech are voiced and during their production the vocal tract exhibits at least two and usually three well-marked resonances, the vowel formants. Table 3 gave some average

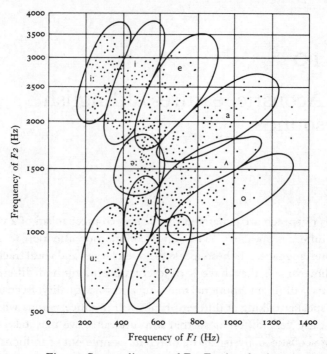

Fig. 42. Scatter diagram of F_1–F_2 plots for American vowels.
(After G. E. Peterson & H. L. Barney, 'Control methods used in a study of the vowels', *Journal of the Acoustical Society of America*, 1952, **24**, 182).

values for the frequency of F_1 and F_2 for eleven English pure vowels. As these are average values, they will not be closely reproduced in the utterances of an individual speaker, but they do show the trends we may expect to see in spectrograms of such utterances. Because the sounds are voiced, wide-band spectrograms will show vertical striations throughout the stretch corresponding to the vowel sound; the presence of the formants will be indicated by broad, dark bars running through the same stretch denoting high levels of energy in certain frequency regions. The spectrograms of Fig. 43 are of utterances in which each word was said in isolation and this accounts for the relatively steady formant bars, somewhat in contrast with those seen in Fig. 41.

As the average values suggest, the progression from close front articulation to open front articulation is marked by the gradual approximation of the bars for F_1 and F_2. With the shift to back articulation, F_1 and F_2 come much closer together and for the five back vowels tend to move downwards together. For the centrally produced

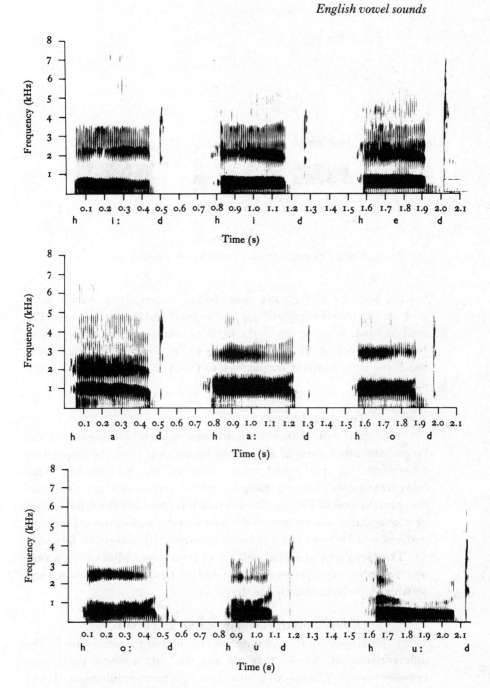

Fig. 43. Spectrograms of English pure vowels [*cont. on p. 114*].

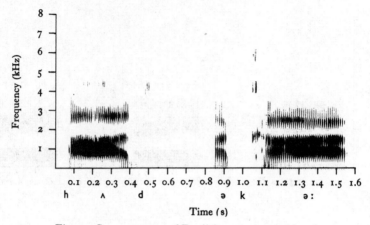

Fig. 43. Spectrograms of English pure vowels [*cont.*]

vowels, both F_1 and F_2 are again higher in frequency, occupying a position between the dispositions for the front and the back vowels. The neutral vowel is not given in the table of average formant frequencies because of its variability; in the example in Fig. 43, it is seen to have very much the same formant frequencies as the stressed vowel of the word *occur*.

The diphthongs

The articulation of diphthongs requires a movement of the tongue and other parts of the speech mechanism from the disposition appropriate for one vowel sound towards that for another. This movement causes a marked change in the formant pattern, as we see from the spectrograms of Fig. 44. In each case it is clear that the syllable does present a combination of two of the pure vowels: *high* shows the formant pattern for [aː] followed by that for [i], *here* shows [i] followed by [ə] and so on. The fact that a syllable made up of semi-vowel plus vowel is very much a diphthong in reverse is illustrated by the spectrograms of *you* and *we* which have been included in the figure.

Differences in vowel duration and intensity

Important though differences in formant structure are for the differentiation of vowels, they are not the only acoustic differences between vowels. The spectrograms show up a further difference, that in duration. A good deal of caution is necessary in deriving values for

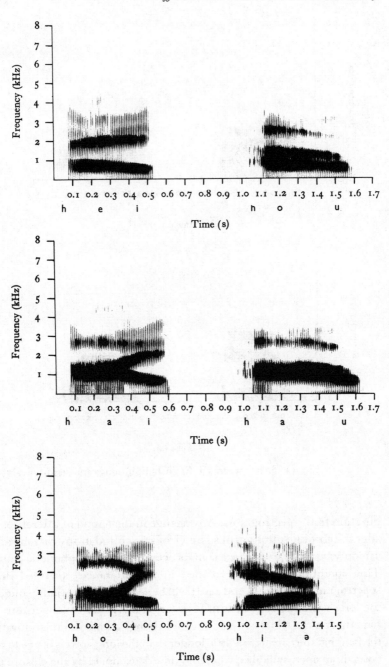

Fig. 44. Spectrograms of English dipthongs and semi-vowels [*cont. on p. 116*].

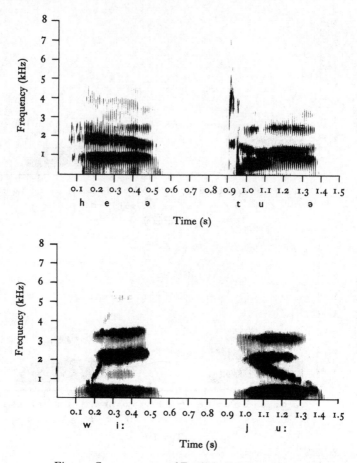

Fig. 44. Spectrograms of English diphthongs and semi-vowels [*cont.*].

duration from spectrograms. Any change in the tempo of utterances will alter the absolute duration of a stretch of speech and in any case durations can only be compared where sounds occur in a similar phonetic context. This condition is largely satisfied in the utterances analysed in the spectrograms of Figs. 43 and 44. It will be seen that the periodic sound for the long vowels, [iː], [aː], [oː], [uː], [əː] is markedly of longer duration than that for the short vowels. The diphthongs are all of similar duration; the fact that they are here a little longer than the long vowels is due to their position in open syllables, where no time is occupied by the closure for a final plosive.

The overall intensity of vowel sounds naturally depends upon the speaking level that is adopted; in fact a change of level from soft to loud, for example, is effected almost entirely through the vowel sounds. If the volume is kept approximately constant, however, there remain intrinsic differences in intensity between the various vowels. As one might expect, vowels made with the vocal tract more open have a higher intensity level than the close vowels; for the same degree of openness, back vowels, in which $F1$ and $F2$ are closer together in frequency, are a little more intense than front vowels. These effects can be seen from the intensity values given in Table 5 (p. 127); the difference between the highest and the lowest intensity vowel sound on average is 7 dB.

English consonant sounds

The sounds which make up the consonant system are of considerably greater diversity than the vowels since they are differentiated not only by place of articulation but by manner, by the use of noise generation and by the voiced–voiceless distinction. In order to review their acoustic characteristics we shall group together sounds which show some similarities of articulation since this means inevitably that they are likely to have acoustic features in common.

The dichotomy vowel-consonant is based on a distinction which cannot be made according to acoustic criteria; it is essentially a matter of the function of sounds in a language system. If, for example, we invoke the notion of noise components as being characteristic of consonant sounds, then in general nasal and lateral sounds would be excluded from the class; on the other hand, it would make no sense to consider that a whispered message involved no vowel sounds, although it consists entirely of noise. From the acoustic point of view, then, there is no sharp line of demarcation between vowel sounds and consonant sounds; there are only sounds which are more like and sounds which are less like the vowels of voiced speech. In English, those which are more like vowels are those which can, understandably enough, have syllabic function, that is the nasal and the lateral consonants.

Nasal consonants

The articulation of nasal sounds involves the lowering of the soft palate so that the air passage which leads out through the nasopharynx and the nostrils is open. The acoustic result of opening what is effectively a side-branch of the vocal tract is to change the resonance

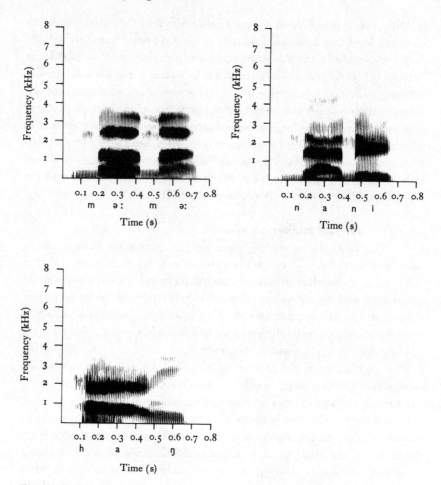

Fig. 45. Spectrograms of syllables containing nasal consonants.

characteristics of the tract and to introduce an anti-resonance, that is a specific filtering effect. The frequency band affected by this anti-resonance is that in which we find the second formant of most vowel sounds, that is from about 800 up to about 2000 Hz. In syllables where a vowel is immediately preceded or followed by a nasal consonant, we see two marked effects of the anti-resonance in the spectrographic pattern: first, the peak of energy produced by F_1 is at a lower frequency in the consonant stretch than in the vowel, and second, there is a more or less sudden change from the high level of energy for the vowel second formant to a very low or zero level of energy for the consonant. These features are clear in the spectrograms of Fig. 45.

In nasal consonants the oral branch of the vocal tract is closed off during the time when the nasal branch is open; the nostrils are less effective than the mouth in radiating sound into the outer air and consequently the overall intensity level of nasal consonants is noticeably lower than that of vowels with which they are associated, as can be seen from the fainter traces in the spectrograms.

A comparison of the various nasal consonants represented in the figure shows that there is very little in the resonance or formant bars to differentiate them; they all have F_I in the lowest frequency band and a second formant at about the frequency of the vowel F_3. The feature which is important for distinguishing the three nasal articulations from each other is to be found in the rapid changes of formant frequency, the formant transitions mentioned in the previous chapter. In the present context the transitions of F_2 are particularly important; the bi-labial articulation, [m], produces a transition of F_2 from or towards a lower frequency, depending upon whether the consonant is initial or final; the alveolar, [n], involves rather little transition and the velar, [ŋ], a transition from or towards a higher frequency. The next chapter will contain a full discussion of the way in which such acoustic features are used in the differentiation of sounds.

The point has already been made that the duration of sounds is a very relative matter and little can be said about the duration of a consonant or even of a class of consonants taken by itself. It may be noted, however, that the English nasals tend to occupy a good proportion of the time allotted to a syllable, as can be seen from some of the examples in Fig. 45; this is particularly the case in consonant clusters where a nasal is followed by a stop consonant.

[l] and [r] sounds

From the spectrograms of Fig. 44 we have seen that the semi-vowels [j] and [w] are glides from the formant disposition for the vowels [i] and [u] respectively towards the formant positions for a following vowel. These glides are formant transitions, changes from one formant frequency to another, but they take place at a rate which is considerably slower than that of the transitions, for example, in a sequence of nasal consonant plus vowel. The latter may occupy about 25 ms whereas the former, at a comparable rate of utterance, require something over 100 ms.

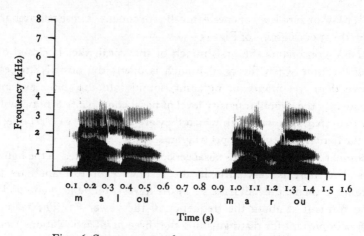

Fig. 46. Spectrograms of *marrow* and *mallow*.

In Southern English, two other classes of sound are acoustically akin to the semi-vowels; these are the most commonly used [r] sound and the [l] sounds. The frictionless [r] is a glide from a neutral vowel, made with some degree of retroflexion, towards a following vowel and is therefore characterized by formant transitions away from and towards a retroflex vowel pattern. An important feature of the [r] pattern is the marked transition in F_3 as well as in F_1 and F_2. This is apparent in the spectrogram of *marrow* shown in Fig. 46, where the intervocalic position of the consonant occasions transitions associated with the preceding and the following vowel. They take place relatively slowly, though a little more rapidly than those for [j] and [w].

This pattern may be compared with that for intervocalic [l] in the word *mallow*. Here the transitions are less extensive and less leisurely than for [r]; this is particularly noticeable in F_1 which has quite abrupt transitions in the intervocalic [l]. The most striking difference, however, lies in F_3 which shows no change of frequency, in contrast to the extensive transition of F_3 in the intervocalic [r] of *marrow*. All transitions are of course determined by the formant frequencies of preceding and following vowel sounds but this F_3 difference between [l] and [r] is maintained in all contexts.

The difference between the clear and dark [l] sounds in English is reflected, as we should expect, in formant differences. It is mainly the disposition of F_1 and F_2 that is affected, clear [l] having formant

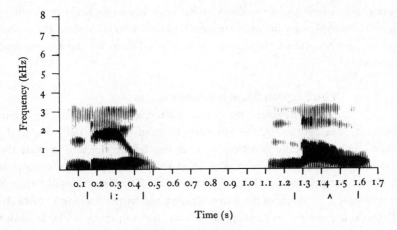

Fig. 47. Spectrograms of *leal* and *lull*.

frequencies appropriate to a front vowel and dark [l] to a back vowel. Clear [l] in most English pronunciations is somewhat influenced by the vowel which it precedes. The spectrograms of the words *leal* and *lull* in Fig. 47 illustrate this point and also show the difference between clear and dark [l].

Friction noise

We turn now to the remainder of the consonant sounds, which are acoustically distinct from the vowels either because of the presence of noise or because they involve a complete interruption of the stream of sound. In the previous chapter we looked at the general character of the spectrographic patterns which correspond to these sounds: noise produces a patch indicating energy randomly distributed over some part of the spectrum; the interruption due to a stop consonant interposes a blank patch in the spectrogram. The extent and position of a noise patch on the frequency axis reflects the filtering effect of the vocal tract; the extent of the noise on the time axis will be greatest for fricative consonants and least for the noise bursts occasioned by the release of a plosive consonant. Affricates show noise of longer duration than the plosive burst but shorter than a fricative in a similar context.

Differences in the intensity of friction noise are very largely a function of the width of the frequency band covered by the noise; the wider the band, the greater the total intensity is likely to be. Some of the differences between a voiced and a voiceless sound have been touched upon; where there is friction noise, its intensity tends to be less in the case of the voiced sound, since some of the energy is being used up by the larynx tone generator.

The English fricative consonants

In order to illustrate typical patterns for the fricatives we shall use examples containing the voiceless member of each pair of sounds, placed in intervocalic position so that the beginning and end of the consonant sound may be seen. Fig. 48 gives spectrograms for five sounds in these conditions: [ʃ], [s], [f], [θ]and [h]. The first four illustrate a progressive narrowing of the noise band passed by the vocal tract filter. In [ʃ] the noise energy begins quite low in the frequency scale, at about 1800–2000 Hz and extends upwards for a considerable distance, to 6000 Hz and beyond. In [s] the filter suppresses most of the noise energy below about 4000 Hz but the band extends upwards to 8000 Hz. Both [f] and [θ] have the main noise energy in the high-frequency band from about 6000 to 8000 Hz.

The [h] sound has a different character from the other fricatives because the noise generator in this case is at the level of the larynx and the sound is more in the nature of a whispered vowel; although it consists of noise, it has marked formant bars which correspond very closely in frequency with the formants of the following vowel sound.

The English plosive consonants

The occurrence of a plosive consonant is marked by a short silence or near-silence followed by a short burst of noise if the stop is released. The duration of these component parts of the sound depends very much upon the tempo of the utterance; the silence is likely to last something between 70 and 140 ms, being shorter in the voiced sounds than in the voiceless. The burst of noise is of very short duration in contexts where the sound has little or no aspiration; here it may last no more than about 10 or 15 ms; where there is marked aspiration, it may be of the order of 50 ms. During the burst the noise energy is spread rather widely over the spectrum but peaks of energy tend to occur at different frequency regions according to the place of articulation of the consonant. In the bi-labial sounds, [p] and [b], the maximum is generally in the low frequencies, at about 600–800 Hz; for the velar sounds it is in the region of 1800–2000 Hz and for the alveolars, in the higher frequencies at about

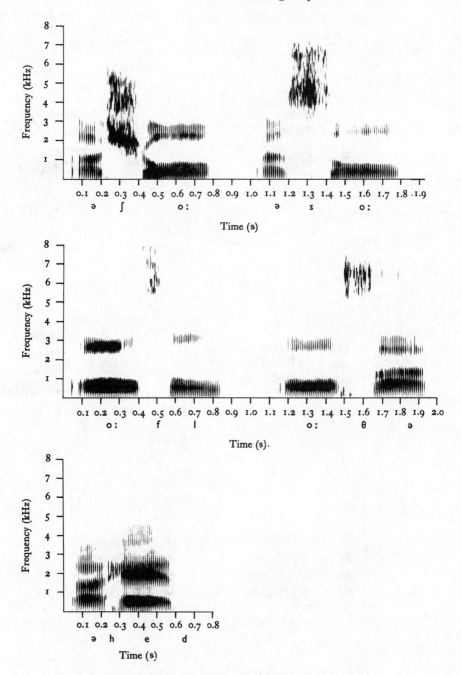

Fig. 48. Spectrograms of English voiceless fricatives, intervocalic.

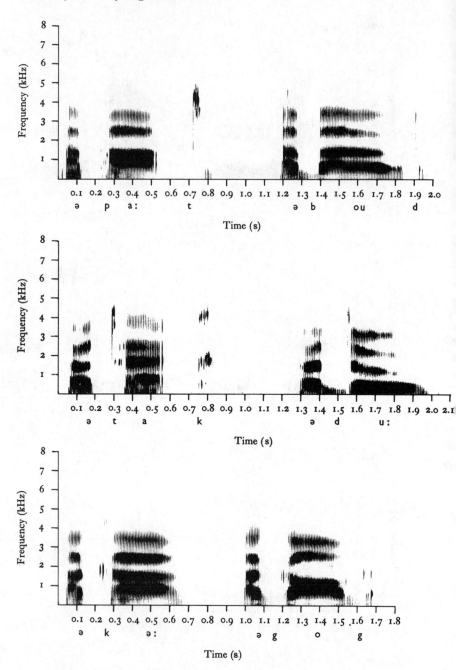

Fig. 49. Spectrograms of English plosives.

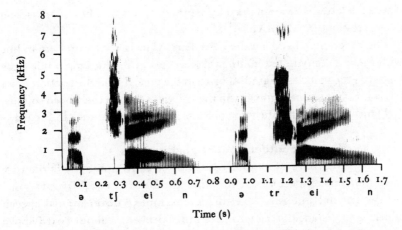

Fig. 50. Spectrograms of English voiceless affricates.

4000 Hz. In the voiced sounds, [b], [d] and [g], the intensity of the noise burst is much less than in the voiceless sounds, [p], [t] and [k]. These various features of the plosive consonants can be seen in the spectrographic examples shown in Fig. 49.

The English affricates

The articulation of an affricate consists in making a complete closure of the vocal tract at some point, as for a plosive consonant, and the production of friction noise at the point where the release occurs. There are only two pairs of affricates in the English sound system and for all four sounds the stop is made well back on the alveolar ridge; in [tʃ] and [dʒ], the initial sounds of *chain* and *Jane*, the friction noise is the same as in *shame*, that is to say the vocal tract filter imposes a lower cut-off to the noise energy at about 1800–2000 Hz. To achieve this condition the closure for the affricate has to be made a little further back than for the simple [t] and [d]. For the other pair of affricates, [tr] and [dr], the initial sounds in *train* and *drain*, the articulation is essentially that of the continuant [r], with the tip of the tongue retroflexed; the stop is therefore made further back still and the friction is a fricative version of [r]. The noise now has a lower cut-off frequency at about 1200 Hz.

The duration of the stop in the affricates tends to be about the same as for a simple plosive in similar position but the friction lasts very much longer than the burst of noise that marks the release of a plosive, even where the latter is accompanied by aspiration; it is not, however, as long as a corresponding fricative.

The differences between the voiced and voiceless affricates are in line with those already noted in other classes of sound. The stop tends to be longer in the voiceless sound, shorter in the voiced, and the friction noise has somewhat greater intensity in the voiceless than in the voiced sounds.

Typical patterns for the two voiceless affricates are shown in Fig. 50.

Relative intensity of English sounds

We have seen that by taking a large number of intensity measurements of speech and computing the mean we can arrive at a value for the general intensity level of, for example, conversational speech which, at a distance of 1 metre from the speaker, is about 60 dB above reference level. When a speaker talks very loudly he raises this average level and when he talks softly it falls by a certain number of decibels. It has been found, however, that the short-term fluctuation in intensity consequent upon the syllabic structure of speech tends to show very much the same pattern for different overall intensity levels; that is to say, if we measure the decibel differences between successive sounds in an utterance, the values remain roughly the same in loud speech, in conversational speech and in quiet speech.

One of the inherent differences between sounds that constitute a language system is evidently that of overall intensity. Since the acoustic distinctions are the result of articulatory movements which vary the dimensions of the vocal tract in a more or less consistent fashion, it is not surprising that the same string of sounds should tend to produce similar fluctuations in intensity. It is therefore possible by taking a large number of intensity measurements to arrive at average values for the intensity differences between sounds corresponding to the phonemic units of the English system. In Table 5 these mean values are given with reference to the intensity of [θ] as in *thin*, which is the English sound with the lowest intensity, and hence no value is assigned to this sound. The average difference in intensity between all other sounds and this reference sound is given in the table in decibels, with the sounds arranged in descending order of intensity.

In any stretch of speech the vowel sounds occupy the major part of the time and are responsible for the higher intensity levels; they therefore make by far the greatest contribution to the long-term average of intensity. If this mean value is, let us say, 60 dB, then the more intense

TABLE 5. *Relative intensity of English sounds (in decibels)*

oː	29	m	17
o	28	tʃ	16
aː	26	n	15
ʌ	26	dʒ	13
əː	25	ʒ	13
a	24	z	12
u	24	s	12
e	23	t	11
i	22	g	11
uː	22	k	11
iː	22	v	10
w	21	ð	10
r	20	b	8
j	20	d	8
l	20	p	7
ʃ	19	f	7
ŋ	18	θ	—

vowel sounds will register a few decibels above this, with [oː] at perhaps 65 dB, and the interspersion of the low-intensity sounds will bring the average down to 60 dB and there will be a similar distribution of levels if the overall intensity is as high as 70 dB or as low as 50 dB. All the vowel sounds therefore come first in the table, with the open vowels first and the close vowels next. The diphthongs, which are not entered in the table, may be taken as having approximately the intensity level of their starting point vowels. After the vowels come the vowel-like sounds, including those which may have syllabic function in English. The considerable width of the noise-band in [ʃ] accounts for its high position in the table. At the other end of the scale, we find the weak fricatives and the plosives. In a single syllable like *thought*, therefore, the listener is faced with a drop of intensity of almost 30 dB.

The information given in this chapter has been chiefly aimed at placing the reader in a position to look at spectrograms of English utterances and to learn the various kinds of acoustic feature that may be detected in them. The illustrations have been deliberately chosen to throw these features into relief and it must be emphasized that spectrograms of running speech, in contrast with isolated words, are by no means as easy to make sense of. It has already been said, too, that speech exhibits great acoustic variability and spectrograms of utterances from different individual speakers will be found to differ very widely. Experience in looking at spectrograms does, however, enable one to pick out essential features, that is features which have the greatest weight in distinguishing one sound from another. As we shall see in the next chapter, not all items of acoustic information are equally important, particularly from the point of view of speech reception.

11

Acoustic cues for the recognition of speech sounds

The point has been made several times that the sounds of speech are extremely variable, that is to say that when a number of different speakers utter the 'same' word, the sounds are acoustically different in many respects. In spite of this it is very rarely that we have any difficulty in recognizing a word spoken to us; as listeners we are very well practised in arriving at the right answer when taking in a message in the face of a wide range of variation in the acoustic signals. Two factors are mainly responsible for our ability to do this: first, whenever someone is talking to us, we have a very good idea of what to expect; from our knowledge of the language, of the person talking and of the general situation we are able to predict more or less the course the message will follow. This property of speech and of language which makes such prediction possible is referred to technically as *redundancy*. Spoken messages also show redundancy in the more everyday sense of the word, they contain a great deal more information than is really needed for the understanding of the message, and this is particularly true at the acoustic level. The sound waves reaching our ears contain frequencies from 30 to 10 000 Hz, they embody intensity variations over a range of 30 dB or more and changes in frequency and intensity are taking place many times a second. We do not in fact need all this acoustic information just to decode the spoken message and the second factor which accounts for our success in dealing with the variability of speech is our capacity for discarding quite a proportion of this information and pinning our attention to a few selected acoustic features. These features we use for diagnostic purposes, for deciding between sound x and sound y, and they are called *acoustic cues*.

The function of acoustic cues

Words are recognized as being made up of a string of phonemes and the first process in taking in speech is the identification of incoming sounds as representing particular phoneme categories. The whole phonemic system of a language, for example the forty-odd phoneme categories of English, operates as a self-consistent system of relations, that is to say recognizing a sound means not simply identifying it as belonging to one phoneme category but deciding that it does not belong to any one of the other 39. An English sound which is classed by a listener in the phoneme /p/ has been recognized as a bi-labial consonant but as being different from /b/, which is also bi-labial but voiced, different from /m/, which is bi-labial but nasal and different from /w/, which is bi-labial but a semi-vowel. It is precisely these relationships which constitute the framework of the phonological system; acoustic cues are used to make decisions about these relationships and hence the cues themselves must depend upon relations between physical quantities and not on absolute values. The clearest example of this principle is the use of formant frequencies as a cue for vowel recognition; a child's vowel formant frequencies are all higher than a man's but we have no hesitation in categorizing a child's vowel sounds in the same way as a man's because we are judging the relations between the formants and not their absolute frequency.

For the identification of any one sound generally several acoustic cues are needed. If we recognize /p/ by distinguishing it from /b/, from /m/ and from /w/, it is not likely that we can do so on the strength of the same item of acoustic information; we shall need a combination of a number of cues in order to arrive at a firm decision that the sound in question belongs to the /p/ category. This does not mean that in every situation we use the same cues or combination of cues; this depends very much on the redundancy of the message, for there may be contexts in which a single acoustic cue is enough to produce a decision.

One further comment on the functioning of acoustic cues is called for: the only necessary qualification for an acoustic cue is that it should enable the listener to make the right decision, that is to recognize correctly the word that has been spoken. So long as this criterion is met, an individual listener may make use of any cues he likes. In fact each one of us evolves his own cues for use in connection with his native language and there is substantial evidence that English listeners, for instance, do not all use the same cues for a given distinction. As one would expect, however, there is also a good deal of common ground among users of one language in this respect and this final chapter will be devoted to a brief review of the acoustic cues known to be used by English listeners. This will be preceded by some account of the experimental method by which this knowledge has been gained.

Experiments on acoustic cues

The speech sound waves which reach our ears embody a lot of information which we do not need for making phonemic decisions. Out of this wealth of data our brain picks the items which it has learned to use for the purpose. Investigation of acoustic cues involves finding out by some means or other what those items are. The invention of the sound spectrograph itself was an attempt in this direction for it was hoped that by making the patterns of speech visible one would throw into relief the features which were really important for recognition. This indeed turned out to be the case and the observations on spectrographic features included in the previous chapter are the basis for most of our notions about acoustic cues, although this term was not in use when spectrography of speech was first carried out on a large scale. Spectrographic analysis does tell us that a certain feature is present in a particular sound and also that the feature tends to recur when the 'same' sound occurs again. It cannot tell us conclusively, however, that listeners are actually using this feature as an acoustic cue, for any speech that we send to them will contain this and many other possible cues as well. In order to obtain firm evidence, we should need to isolate a given cue and see whether it influenced listeners' decisions. The means of doing exactly this has been developed through the use of *speech synthesizers.*

A speech synthesizer is a device which produces speech-like sounds without the aid of a human larynx or vocal tract. A number of different methods have been invoked for the purpose but basically all of them employ electronic circuits which generate electrical impulses which can be converted into sound waves. In an earlier chapter we saw that any speech sound could be constructed from a mixture of sine waves. Electronic circuits are a convenient way of generating sine waves, and therefore with enough circuits we can set up any required mixture; one of the earliest speech synthesizers did in fact make use of this principle. Later devices have used, in preference, circuits to generate a complex tone and a noise, thus mimicking the sound sources of human speech, and filters to reproduce the effects of the vocal tract.

The essential feature of the speech synthesizer is that all the dimensions of the speech-like sound can be controlled by the experimenter; that is to say the frequency, intensity and the time course

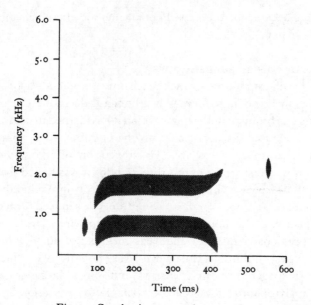

Fig. 51. Synthesizer control pattern for the syllable *bag*.

of all the components in the sound can be regulated within quite close limits. This means first of all that the experimenter knows exactly what acoustic information is being transmitted to listeners and second that this information can be modified in any required direction and to any extent, so that the consequent changes in the listeners' responses can be observed.

The principle can best be appreciated by looking at a spectrogram of the kind of simplified sound which can be used for experiments of this nature. Many of the classic experiments on acoustic cues were in fact carried out with a speech synthesizer designed to 'read' spectograms, that is to say it generated speech-like sounds whose characteristics were controlled by a spectrographic pattern; if this pattern was as complicated as a real spectrogram of speech, then the sounds produced were very like those of real speech. It would also generate sounds in response to very much simplified patterns of the kind shown in Fig. 51. When actuated by this pattern the synthesizer produced a syllable which was easily recognized by English listeners as the word *bag*; the two bars generate formant frequencies appropriate to the vowel, the short bursts of sound at the beginning and the end of the pattern simulate the release of the plosives [b] and [g], the changes of formant frequency provide the necessary formant transitions and the blank space before the final burst interposes the stop of the [g] sound. From the experimental point of view the importance of such sounds is that they can be treated as speech and recognized by listeners and yet it is clear from the spectrogram that the acoustic information they supply has been drastically simplified in comparison with human speech. So much so that it is feasible to manipulate just one acoustic cue and to measure the effect of variations in this cue upon the judgments of listeners.

The function of an acoustic cue, as we said earlier, is to enable the listener to make a distinction between sounds belonging to different phonemic classes. The experimental technique is first to select a possible cue for a particular distinction. This can be done only on the basis of acoustic analysis of natural speech and usually through the study of spectrograms. By inspecting a great many spectrograms we may discover, for example, that when a plosive consonant is released the resulting burst of noise has a major peak of energy at some place on the frequency scale and that the location of this peak tends to vary systematically according to the point of articulation of the sound, that is whether it is bi-labial, alveolar or velar. With the aid of the speech synthesizer we can set up a whole series of syllables in which an initial burst of noise is made to vary from a low frequency, let us say with the centre frequency of the burst at 300 Hz, up to a high frequency, with the centre frequency at 3600 Hz. Our analytical data tell us that with such a range of variation the sounds produced may be expected to cover all the three classes, /b/, /d/ and /g/. To explore the effect of this cue we need to present all the various stimuli to groups of listeners and ask them to say in each case whether they hear the syllable as beginning with /b/, with /d/ or with /g/. In such a listening test it is important that the stimuli should be presented in random order and it is usual for each stimulus to occur several times.

This was one of the first experiments to be carried out with a speech synthesizer. A range of plosive bursts was combined with a two-formant sound having the quality of [a]; the formants were straight bars, without transitions of the kind seen in Fig. 51 since these would have acted as a second cue for the listeners. The results of the experiment showed that when the centre frequency of the burst was low, up to about 500 Hz, there was agreement among the listeners that the syllable began with /b/; when the burst was at a mid-frequency, from about 1200–2000 Hz, the syllables were heard to begin with /g/, and when it was high, from about 3100 Hz upwards, it began with /d/. Across the intervening ranges, from 500 to 1200 Hz and from 2000 to 3100 Hz, there was disagreement among listeners, showing that these are areas of uncertainty between one phonemic category and the neighbouring one.

Information such as this about the operation of acoustic cues in speech could not be obtained simply through the acoustic analysis of natural speech. Analysis is a necessary starting point since it is the only way in which possible cues can be found; speech synthesis is an indispensable complement, however, because it affords the only means of testing conclusively whether a given cue is actually employed by listeners. The technique has been used to explore the cues for various types of sound and the results of much of this work will be summarized in the following sections. It must be borne in mind that this is a summary and therefore many details are omitted. The whole process of speech communication is extremely complex and the operation of acoustic cues is by no means the least complex part of it. The aim is to give general indications as to the way in which acoustic cues work. The point has already been made that a cue is a means of making a particular distinction, not of identifying a sound as belonging to a given phoneme; the latter requires the combination of a number of distinctions and inevitably there is interaction between the effect of one cue and another. In dealing with each category of sounds, we shall note the various differentiations that may be involved and the cues that tend to have a bearing on these distinctions.

Acoustic cues for vowel differentiation

As far as the recognition of vowel sounds is concerned there is not a great deal that needs to be added to what was said in the earlier chapters. When we listen to the speech of a stranger we rapidly erect for ourselves a frame of reference against which we differentiate his vowel qualities; with a familiar speaker, we have the reference frame ready stored in our brain and bring it into operation when he speaks. The principal cue on which these frames are based is the relation of the F_1 and F_2 frequencies, or more exactly the relations of these relations. This is the information which is embodied, for example, in the plots of Fig. 33. The vowel sounds of an individual speaker form a system which will occupy a set of locations in that F_1–F_2 space. In a child's speech, the frame will be further down and to the left and in a man with a long vocal tract, further up and to the right. A few seconds' listening enables us to establish these facts and we then recognize the sounds within the system on the basis of the F_1–F_2 cue.

Although the formant cue has the greatest weight it is not the only one available to us in differentiating vowel sounds. In most types of English there is a duration cue which distinguishes those vowels which tend to be long from those which tend to be short, but the distribution of the two classes varies with the dialect. In Southern English the vowels of *heed*, *had*, *hard*, *hoard*, *who'd* and *heard* generally have greater duration than those in *hid*, *head*, *hod*, *Hudd* and *hood*. The dipthongs fall into the class of long vowels.

Finally, there is an intensity cue which helps to differentiate at least the open vowels from the close vowels, particularly in situations where there is any considerable level of masking noise. The total range of variation is only about 7 dB but this cue makes some contribution to vowel recognition.

Acoustic cues for the voiced–voiceless distinction

In the English consonant system the distinction between voiced and voiceless articulation plays a part in nine pairs of sounds in all. The cues for the differentiation are common to all the pairs in spite of other differences in manner and place of articulation and it will therefore be well to deal with this set of cues first.

The terms *voiced* and *voiceless* imply either the presence or absence of vocal fold vibration during the articulation of the sound and in some contexts this contrast is maintained. For most English speakers this is only when the consonant sounds occur in intervocalic position; here it usually happens that vocal fold vibration is continued throughout the articulation of the voiced member of the pair of sounds but ceases for an appreciable time in the production of the voiceless sound. In such cases an acoustic cue for the distinction is the presence of low-frequency energy, in the voiced sound, in the range occupied by larynx vibration and the continuation of periodicity which is tied to the larynx frequency; the absence of these features is the cue for the voiceless sound.

Where the consonants are either initial or final in a group, however, the production of the voiced sound is not accompanied by larynx vibration throughout its whole duration and other cues have to be employed in making the necessary differentiation. The first of these acoustic cues is connected with larynx activity but in a rather different way. Let us take the example of an initial stop consonant, the contrast between *par* and

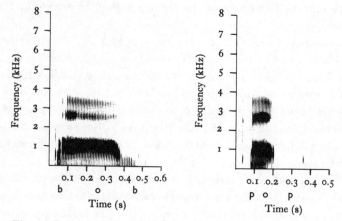

Fig. 52. Spectrograms of *bob* and *pop*.

bar. At some moment during the articulation of both these syllables there will be a burst of noise marking the release of the plosive; equally, at some moment vocal fold vibration will begin for the periodic sound. In the syllable beginning with /b/, the inception of vibration will be simultaneous or very nearly simultaneous with the noise burst; in the syllable with initial /p/, there is a time interval between the burst and the beginning of larynx vibration, an interval which will be of the order of 50–70 ms. The start of vocal fold vibration viewed in relation to the noise burst or some other articulatory event is referred to as *voice onset time* or VOT; it has been found to constitute an important cue for the voiced–voiceless distinction, not only in English but in a number of other languages.

When stop consonant sounds occur in final position in English we cannot simply reverse the VOT observation, for two reasons: first, the voiced sound very rarely continues larynx vibration up to the moment of the noise burst, and second, with many speakers the final stop sounds are not released at all. Nonetheless the voiced–voiceless distinction is still cued by reference to larynx action; in a syllable closed by a voiced sound, such as *bob*, the periodic sound corresponding to the vowel has longer duration, the stop itself is correspondingly shorter and the larynx vibration continues at least into the beginning of the stop; with the voiceless sound, as in *pop*, the vowel part is shorter, the stop is longer and larynx vibration ceases at the moment when the stop is made. These cues and also the VOT cue can therefore be generalized by saying that with the voiced member of a pair of sounds, vocal fold vibration begins earlier and persists later, while for the voiceless member, it begins later and ends earlier. The presence of these cues for the distinction can be checked by reference to the spectrograms of Fig. 52 where *bob* is contrasted with *pop*. The cues formulated in this more general way are also applicable to the voiced–voiceless distinction in the case of affricates and fricatives.

One further cue for the voiced–voiceless distinction was mentioned in the previous chapter: this is the fact that any noise attendant upon consonant production will have greater intensity in the voiceless sound than in the voiced, whether it be the noise burst at the release of a plosive or the friction noise for an affricate or a fricative. Vocal fold vibration uses up a proportion of the energy available for producing a syllable; the less energy used in this way, the more there is to be dissipated in noise generation, so that in the voiceless sound the noise is of higher intensity and also lasts longer.

Acoustic cues for manner of articulation

Whether a sound is voiced or voiceless is itself one aspect of the manner in which it is produced, but the term is most often applied to the differentiation between plosive, affricate, fricative, nasal, lateral and semi-vowel sounds. Each of these classes of sound affords cues which are self-evident from the spectrographic features already mentioned and they can therefore be summarized quite briefly.

The cue for the plosive class is the interruption in the stream of sound, the silence or near-silence lasting anything from about 40 to about 120 ms in running speech. Only one other class of sound shares this cue and that is the affricate class, in which the duration of the silence is comparable but which is differentiated by greater duration of the noise component. The cue for affricates and fricatives, then, is the presence of noise of appreciable duration, from about 70 to 140 ms.

Nasals, laterals and semi-vowels are distinguished from the previous three classes by the absence of noise and the presence of continuous tone. Nasals are cued by a low-frequency resonance and the absence of energy between this frequency band and a band beginning in the region of 2000 Hz. Laterals and semi-vowels are marked by vowel-like formants with relatively slow variations in formant frequency, the transitions being, however, more rapid in the laterals than the semi-vowels.

137

Acoustic cues for place of articulation

The effect of the cues indicated so far is to enable the listener to reduce to a comparatively small class the possible identifications of any sound he is processing. In order to be in a position to reduce this still further to a single solution, he has to be able to differentiate sounds produced at various points in the vocal tract. We have seen that changes in vocal tract shape affect the resonance or filtering effects of the tract and the cues for place of articulation must therefore be related to these changes in the filter conditions. Speech is continuous movement; some movements are made rapidly, others more slowly; some involve comparatively large distances, as at the beginning of the word *thought*, others smaller distances, as in the word *tea*. The distance and the speed of the movements are reflected in the rate and the extent of the acoustic changes, principally the changes in formant frequency and in the noise filtering, and it is indeed here that we find the major cues for place of articulation.

The second formant transition cue

All formant transitions carry information which can be used by the listener, but it has been found by experiment that transitions of the second formant are particularly liable to be used as a cue for place of articulation. When a plosive sound is released there is a very rapid acoustic change which is reflected in quick changes in formant frequency affecting all the formants since one set of resonances of the vocal tract has been transformed into another set in a short space of time. The influence of the resulting F_2 transitions on what the listener perceives can best be seen by reference to the simplified spectrograms of Fig. 53. These form a series of patterns used in producing synthesized syllables. The 14 patterns differ from each other in one respect only, the F_2 transition. In stimulus 1 this is an extensive transition from a frequency well below that of the steady-state formant; in the middle of the series, at stimulus 8, there is zero transition and at stimulus 14 the F_2 transition is an extensive fall from a higher frequency. Each syllable lasts for 300 ms and the F_1 transition is constant throughout, so that only one feature of the sound is varied. When these syllables are presented to listeners in random order they experience no difficulty in identifying each one of them as one of the English words *bay*, *day* or *gay* (although the patterns give no cue for the diphthongization of the vowel). There is very general agreement that the stimuli numbered 1 and 2 begin with /b/, numbers 6 and 7 begin with /d/

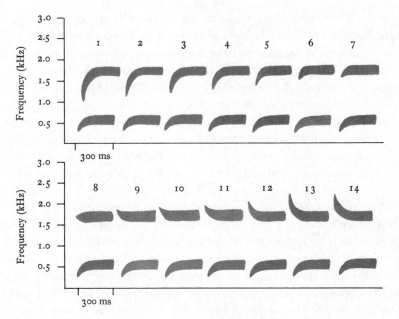

Fig. 53. Synthesizer control patterns for F_2 transition stimuli.

and numbers 13 and 14 with /g/. It is evident that the F_2 transition is an effective cue for the place of articulation of a plosive consonant.

If these patterns are laterally reversed so that the transitions occur at the end instead of at the beginning of the steady-state formants, then each syllable is heard to end with a plosive. Stimulus number 1 would then have a falling F_2 transition, number 14 a rising transition and so on. To avoid the confusion attendant on the use of the terms rising and falling in this context, it is customary to speak of a *minus* transition when the change is either towards or away from a frequency lower than that of the steady-state formant and a *plus* transition when it is towards or away from a higher frequency.

Transitions cannot of course be independent of the vowel formants with which they are associated. The F_2 transition cue for place of articulation is influenced as to the degree and to some extent the direction of the transition by the frequency of the steady-state F_2. This affects mainly the cue for the alveolar place of articulation; it can be said with a good degree of generality that bi-labial articulation entails a minus F_2 transition and velar articulation, a plus F_2 transition. F_2 transitions of small extent, either minus or plus, cue the alveolar place of articulation.

If the F_2 transition cue is truly a cue for place of articulation, then it must operate for other manners of articulation besides the plosive, and this has proved to be the case. The English sound system includes nasal consonants with the same points of articulation as the plosives and the F_2 transition cue works in the same way for these. The resonances referred to earlier as indicating the nasal manner of articulation only inform the listener that he is dealing with a nasal consonant; they do not by themselves enable him to distinguish among the bi-labial, alveolar and velar nasal sounds. For this purpose he needs the F_2 transition cue; if the transition is minus, the nasal sound is /m/, if it is plus, it is /ŋ/ and if it is small in extent or zero, the sound is /n/.

We have spoken so far of only three points of articulation, bi-labial, alveolar and velar but it will be clear that any movement within the vocal tract is likely to generate a transition which is a potential cue for the listener. The relatively slow transitions which we have seen in the case of the semi-vowels provide place information, the plus transition in /j/ showing palatal articulation and the minus transition in /w/, velar articulation. In other types of sound the F_2 place cue may be used in conjunction with other cues or may be largely replaced by them, as tends to happen in the case of fricatives.

Noise filtering cue for place of articulation

When noise is generated in the vocal tract, the filtering of the noise is determined partly by the location of the noise generator and consequently a further cue to place is the perceptual impression made by the noise. This fact lies behind the experiment mentioned in a previous section on the frequency band of the noise burst in plosive consonants. Bi-labial articulation leads to a filtering of the plosive noise such as to produce a peak in the low frequencies, alveolar articulation produces a high-frequency peak and velar articulation a mid-frequency peak. In plosives therefore this noise filtering cue is always present if the plosive is released, in addition to the F_2 transition cue; it may well play a considerable part in the recognition of these consonants, particularly of the voiceless sounds, where the noise burst has greater intensity.

For the group of English sounds which includes the fricatives and the affricates, the noise filtering cue indicates place of articulation by progressively higher cut-off of the noise as the point of articulation moves further forward in the tract; the sounds are in other words progressively higher pitched. The friction noise in the affricates /tr/ and /dr/ is the lowest pitched, having a cut-off at about 1200 Hz; then come /ʃ/ and /ʒ/, with the corresponding affricates, having a cut-off at about 1800 Hz, /s/ and /z/, cut-off at about 4000 Hz and finally the most forward of the fricative articulations, /θ/ and /ð/ and /f/ and /v/, all with a cut-off at approximately 6000 Hz. The noise filtering cue is not sufficient to determine the place of articulation for the last group and it has to be combined with the *F2* transition cue.

Speech reception and the combination of acoustic cues

The principal aim of this last chapter has been to give as far as possible a realistic impression of the use to which a listener puts the stream of acoustic information which reaches him when someone is talking. It is most important to realize that the use of acoustic cues, the actual hearing of speech sounds, is only one part of the infinitely complex process of speech reception. When we take in speech, we hear just enough to provide a rough scaffolding on which we reconstruct the message which the speaker is probably sending us. Our knowledge of the language combined with a great deal of guessing and prediction enable us to carry out this work of reconstruction successfully but as a basis for it we have to recognize a proportion of the sounds that come in and to assign them correctly to their phonemic categories. It is here that we rely on the acoustic cues which we habitually use and we are always using them in combination. The cues for place of articulation, for voicing, for manner of production, the frequency cues, the intensity cues and the time cues are all being applied together and their function is to allow us to eliminate all solutions except the correct one. The weight we give to all the various cues changes with the sequence and the situation; an increase in the surrounding noise may make some cues unusable and throw others into prominence; an unlikely word may cause us to revise completely our notions of what may come next and make us seize every acoustic cue that is available.

Little has been said specifically about the cues needed for the processing of the rhythm and intonation of a spoken message. In addition to the phonemic decoding that is going on, the brain is all the time attending to the fluctuations in intensity, the variations in larynx frequency and the temporal patterns presented by the succession of syllables in order to arrive at the rhythm and intonation, which have such important implications for the decoding of the message. All these various strands of the process are followed at the same time, in parallel, and it is only long practice that renders the brain capable of the continuous work of audition, prediction and revision which enables it to transform the infinitely complex and variable sound waves of speech into a sequence of words, phrases and sentences. The fact that millions of human beings are busy performing this feat at every minute of the day does not make the transformation any less remarkable.

INDEX

Index

damping, 73
frequency response, 73
length, 72
noise filter, 87–8
output, 74–5
resonances, 72–3, 85, 97
voice
average fundamental frequency, 68
child's, 68
creaky, 68
pitch, 68
quality, 69, 70
woman's, 68
voice onset time (VOT), 136
voiced sounds, 69, 86, 108
voiced–voiceless distinction, 135–7
voiceless sounds, 69, 103, 108
vowel(s)
back, 78, 113
central, 79, 114
close, 113, 127
differentiation, 134–5
formants, 79, 111–12, 113–14
front, 78, 113
open, 78, 113

water
sound velocity in, 36
waves in, 28
watts, 91
waveform, 15, 17, 20, 27, 47, 89
larynx tone, 65
non-repeating, 83, 84
repeating, 22, 82
symmetrical, 23
wavelength, 32–3, 36, 41, 45, 47
wave-motion, 28
in air column, 46
in stretched rope, 29, 37
in stretched string, 43, 45, 47
wave(s)
damped, 26, 38
glottal, 63–9
longitudinal, 31
pulse, 62, 65
reflected, 38, 39, 42
sine, 15, 17: addition of, 21, 22, 46, 65
standing, 39–42, 44, 47
transverse, 30, 44
travelling, 28, 29, 40–2
triangular, 65

whisper, 84, 85, 103
white noise, 85, 87
woman's voice, 68
woodwind instruments, 46, 48, 56
words cited:
bag, 132
bar, 136
bay, 138
began, 108
bob, 136, 137
book, 108
chain, 125
day, 138
drain, 125
gay, 138
had, 78, 79, 135
hard, 78, 79, 85, 135
head, 79, 135
heard, 135
heed, 78, 79, 85, 135
herb, 79
here, 79, 114
hid, 79, 135
high, 114
hoard, 79, 85, 135
hod, 79, 135
hood, 79, 85, 135
how, 79
hub, 79
Hudd, 135
Jane, 125
leal, 121
lull, 121
mallow, 120
marrow, 120
occur, 114
par, 135
pop, 136, 137
read, 108
seashore, 104, 106
shame, 125
she, 108
tea, 138
thin, 126
thought, 127, 138
to, 108
train, 125
we, 114
who, 79
who'd, 135